A LIFE IN COLOR — AN ANXIETY WORKBOOK

Proven CBT Skills and Mindfulness Techniques to Keep Always With You in an Emergency Situation. Overcome Anxiety, Depression, and Panic Attacks.

REBECCA THOMPSON

© Copyright 2020 - All Rights Reserved

The content within this book may not be reproduced, duplicated, or transmitted without direct written permission from the author or the publisher.

Under no circumstances will any blame or legal responsibility be held against the publisher, or author, for any damages, reparation or monetary loss due to the information contained within this book, either directly or indirectly.

Legal Notice

This book is copyright protected. This book is only for personal use. You cannot amend, distribute, sell, use, quote or paraphrase any part, or the content within this book, without the consent of the author or publisher.

Disclaimer Notice

Please note the information contained within this document is for educational and entertainment purposes only. All effort has been executed to present accurate, up-to-date and reliable, complete information. No warranties of any kind are declared or implied. Readers acknowledge that the author is not engaging in the rendering of legal, financial, medical or professional advice. The content within this book has been derived from various sources. Please consult a licensed professional before attempting any techniques outlined in this book.

By reading this document, the reader agrees that under no circumstances is the author responsible for any losses, direct or indirect, which are incurred as a result of the use of the information contained within this document, including, but not limited to,—errors, omissions, or inaccuracies.

Table of Contents

Introduction 6
Chapter 1 Different types of Mindfulness Techniques 8
  Concentration Meditation... 8
  Mindfulness Meditation.. 8
  Everyday Ways to Practice Meditation 10
  Mindfulness-Based Stress Reduction (MBSR) 11
Chapter 2 How to Prepare for Meditation 12
  1: Select a Convenient Time 12
  2: Select a Quiet Place 12
  3: Decide on the Duration of Your Meditation 13
  4: Wear Comfortable Clothes 14
  5: Employ a Comfortable Posture 14
  6: Have a Relatively Empty Stomach 15
  7: Begin With a Few Warm-ups 15
  8: Take Time to Breathe in and Out 17
  9: Maintain a Gentle Smile on Your Face 18
  10: Open Your Eyes Gently and Slowly 18
  11: Prepare Your Mind for Meditation 18
    -Listening to sounds 19
    -Awareness of energy in and out your body 19
    -Be well-rested 20
Chapter 3 Effective Mindfulness Meditations 21
  Mindful Breathing 21
    Be aware 23
    Be present 25
    In the Moment 27
  Mindful Relaxation 29
  Mindfulness Meditation to Find Calm 37
  Mindful Morning Meditation... 40

- Mindful Visualization 44
- Refreshing Mind & Body 47
- Eating With Meaning 50

Chapter 4 The Light Warrior Meditation 56

Chapter 5 The Safe Place Meditation 74

Chapter 6 Changing Maladaptive Thinking With CBT ... 90
- The Main Goal of CBT 91
- Effective Considerations for The Assessment 93
- Intervention & Treatment Analysis 97
- The Power of CBT to Destroy Negative Feelings 101

Chapter 7 Mountain Meditation 103
- Let's get started! 104

Chapter 8 Meditation to Achieve Your Life Goals 118
- Focus Without Judging 120
- Basic Operations 122
- It's All About Focus 122

Chapter 9 Guided Meditation to End Anxiety Attacks ... 123
- Meditative Guide to End Anxiety Attacks 124

Chapter 10 Guided Meditation for Super Motivation 130
- Meditative Guide for Super Motivation 131

Chapter 11 Guided Meditation to Help With Stress Relief 136
- Meditative Guide to Help With Stress Relief 136

Chapter 12 Meditation to Calm the Mind 143
- Common Practices 144
  - How it helps 147

Chapter 13 Meditation of The Present Love 156
- Let's Get Started! 157

Chapter 14 Mantra-Based Meditation 168
- Basic Operations 169
- Your Objective 171

Separating Your Mental and Emotional Processes 172

Chapter 15 How to Visualize a Better Version of Yourself 175

Basic Operations 177

Turbocharge Your Results With Immersive 3D Effects 179

This Method's Best-Selling Point: Experiencing a Creative Explosion 180

Practice, practice, practice 180

Chapter 16 Breath Counting 181
Mental Focus 182

Breaking Free From Your Tendency to Judge 183

Taming the Reactive Mind 184

Chapter 17 Anxiety and Stress Relief Scripts 186

Chapter 18 The Road to Healing 199
Managing Symptoms 200

Moving Forward 206

Conclusion 212

Introduction

Even though anxiety can be hard to manage, people should not feel like they have to struggle with it forever. The first step to recovery is often to acknowledge its many symptoms like sweating, trembling, a racing heart, and nervousness. Making efforts not to let anxious thoughts control your day and decisions can be difficult, but it can help to keep you from having panic attacks. Learning how to ride out the symptoms of anxiety and panic takes a lot of practice, and it is important not to get discouraged or start avoiding situations because of anxiety.

Sometimes dealing with anxiety can be too much for someone to handle without professional help. It can be difficult to admit what seems like defeat and call a doctor, but it can be the best way for people with severe symptoms to find relief. There is a wide array of options to choose from when picking a doctor. If a person is too overwhelmed by their choices, they can always go to their primary care doctor who can then refer them to a trusted psychologist or counselor.

After establishing a relationship with the therapist, you can then work on establishing trust and working toward a long-term goal with milestones along the way.

Therapists will sometimes recommend meditation as a supplement to other activities that help alleviate anxiety. Exercises such as mindfulness and yoga can help someone take a step back from their negative thoughts and find a moment to calm themselves down. This can give them a chance to rationally work through their anxious thoughts and calm their bodies before panic sets in. The key to reaping the benefits of meditation is to do it regularly and focus on releasing negative thoughts and replacing them with positive attitudes.

Chapter 1 Different types of Mindfulness Techniques

Concentration Meditation

This technique entails focusing on a single point. This could involve watching your breath, repeating a mantra or a single word, staring at a candle flame, counting beads on a rosary or listening to a repetitive song.

In concentration meditation, you simply refocus your awareness on your chosen object of attention every time you find your mind wandering. Instead of chasing after random thoughts, you simply release them. This practice eventually improves your ability to concentrate.

Mindfulness Meditation

Also known as insight meditation, mindfulness encourages you to observe wandering thoughts as they flow through your mind. Your intention is not to interfere with or judge your thoughts but just to be aware of them coming in going out of your mind.

Mindfulness helps you see the general patterns of your thoughts and feelings. Over time, you begin to understand your natural tendencies to quickly judge what you go through as pleasant or unpleasant (good or bad). As you practice mindfulness, you develop inner balance.

Mindfulness meditation was adopted from the traditional practices of Buddhist meditation predominantly the vipassana meditation, which will be discussed later on. Mindfulness meditation is a collective term for the class of techniques used in creating insight and awareness by observation, practicing focused attention and accepting what arises without judging. Although mindfulness meditation incorporates practices and philosophies from the traditions of the Buddhists, the way and style in which it is taught appeals to many from other different cultures and religions.

This is the most popular meditation technique in the West due to open philosophy and its simple nature.

Everyday Ways to Practice Meditation

You shouldn't let the notion of meditating the "right way" increase your stress or anxiety levels. If you prefer to, you can be part of a meditation center or group classes managed by trained instructors. However, you can also practice meditation just on your own. As a beginner, you might find it hard to focus your mind. To deal with this problem, start with a few minutes and then increase your duration gradually.

Moreover, you don't have to be formal about meditation; you could be informal if you like. What's most important is to choose whichever approach you think fits your lifestyle. That's not all; you can integrate meditation into your daily routine like so many people have. For instance, you can start each day with an hour of meditation. Or simply regularly spare some few minutes of your time to meditate- which is perfectly fine.

Mindfulness-Based Stress Reduction (MBSR)

Mindfulness-based stress reduction is a program that combines yoga and mindfulness meditation with science and western medicine, and it takes 8 weeks. Jon Kabat-Zinn created the program in 1979 after his several years of experience in yoga and Buddhism.

He combined his background in science and those teachings to design this whole program that helps people manage illnesses, stress, chronic pain, and anxiety. Jon made people understand that you need not be Buddhist to take up meditation. He went on to make the program pleasant to all people and made it highly accessible. Now, MBRS courses are offered at universities, medical centers, clinics, and hospitals around the world.

Chapter 2 How to Prepare for Meditation

1: Select a Convenient Time

Meditation is an essential relaxation time, so it should be done at a time that is entirely convenient for you. You should select a time that you are sure nothing or nobody is likely to disturb you and that you are free to enjoy and relax.

The most ideal period to practice meditation is during the hours of dawn and dusk. This is because, at these times, it is usually quiet and peaceful, which means getting relaxed and meditating is likely to be easier.

2: Select a Quiet Place

The same way you select a convenient time is the same way you should select a peaceful place where you are likely to execute your meditation without disturbance. You should switch off your phone or set it to silent mode. If helpful at first, listen to music; you should select gentle tunes that will enhance the meditation trance. You can practice your meditation in your home, in the back yard, or a peaceful park.

The peaceful and calm environment is sure to make the experience of meditating more relaxing and enjoyable for a beginner.

3: Decide on the Duration of Your Meditation

Before you begin meditating, you should know how long your session is going to take. It is recommended to have two twenty-minute-long sessions in a day, but it is just important to start as a beginner. One five-minute-long session in a day is just fine.

Whatever time you choose to be meditating, try to be meditating at that exact time every single day to build a habit. Try to make meditation a permanent part of your daily schedule. Youshould stick to the time frame you have decided and don't stop just because you think or feel that it is not working. It certainly takes practice and time to meditate effortlessly. Don't beat yourself up. The most important thing is not to give up and keep up.

Do not check the time during meditation. This is going to interfere with your session. Instead, you should consider setting an alarm to notify you that the time of your practice is up.

4: Wear Comfortable Clothes

Staying calm and focused might be difficult to achieve if you are physically not comfortable due to restrictive or tight clothing. When practicing meditation, ensure you wear loose clothing.

5: Employ a Comfortable Posture

The posture you use also influences your meditation experience. Ensure that the posture you select makes you feel comfortable, steady, and relaxed. Throughout the process, you are required to sit and have your spine in an erect position, keep your neck and shoulders relaxed and keep your eyes closed. What's important is that your torso is balanced and you feel relaxed and comfortable.

There is a common meditation myth that you must be seated in the lotus position while meditating.

Well, so long as you keep your body posture as mentioned above, you are good to go. I choose to sit on a cushion but find what works best for you.

6: Have a Relatively Empty Stomach

The best time to meditate is two hours after having your meal or before eating a meal. But then again, do not push yourself to meditate when you feel really hungry. If you meditate while you're hungry, you will find it quite difficult to focus because of the hunger cramps and you might find yourself thinking about food for the whole session.

7: Begin With a Few Warm-ups

When preparing to begin meditation, it is important to perform a few yoga exercises or warm-ups before sitting down. The following are the yoga poses you can do before meditating:

- ***Hand walking meditation***: Kneel down and place your left and right palm on the floor. Move the left hand, then the right followed by your left leg and then the right.

- ***Find balance on all fours***: Take time to notice how the weight transfers to your hands as you move forward. Move around, now transfer all the weight to your left hand and knee, then to your right back and forward. Settle into equal weights slowly on all fours.

- ***Cow pose***: Lift your chest and seat while on your inhaling breath as you simultaneously drop your spine towards the floor.

- ***Cat pose***: Reverse the cow pose by exhaling and lifting your waist and dropping your head. With each breath, reverse the curve for 5-10 times. You should do this at a slow pace to feel the spine as it rounds up one way and curves the other way.

- ***Standing up***: Move your left hand back towards your knees, then right and shift to your feet so that you stand up.

This helps in that it gets rid of inertia and restlessness, improves circulation, and helps your body to feel lighter. It also helps in relaxing your mind instead of concentrating on the places you feel sore.

You should stretch your shoulders and neck if you had been seated for a long time. Remember to stretch your lower back and legs as well.

Never miss out on this step as it enables you to sit still for a longer time.

8: Take Time to Breathe in and Out

In easy meditation, taking deep breaths is quite important. In addition to breathing in and out, you should also do some Nadi Shodhan pranayama (alternate nostril breathing) before meditation. You go about Nadi Shodhan pranayama by blocking each nostril in an alternating manner. Doing this is significant in that it channels air in a concentrated flow throughout your body. It also balances energy through your whole body and harmonizes the right and left-brain hemispheres thus easing anxiety and stress. This way, your mind is steered to a calm meditative state and your breathing rhythm is steadied.

9: Maintain a Gentle Smile on Your Face

You are sure to notice an impact when you meditate with a gentle smile on your face. Keeping the smile throughout the meditation session keeps you peaceful, relaxed, and enhances the meditation experience.

10: Open Your Eyes Gently and Slowly

When you near the end of your meditation session, you should not open your eyes in haste or start moving about immediately. You should take time to allow your mind to come back to where you are at the moment and to be aware of yourself then slowly open your eyes.

11: Prepare Your Mind for Meditation

For meditation to be most effective, it is a major requirement to have both your body and mind relaxed so that you can access the deep meditation trance state. As you advance in your meditation experiences, you gain the ability to achieve and maintain trance states even in the presence of distractions. Your mind grows stronger and is able to remain focused but according to your will. Remaining collected, cool and calm even in distractive environments is one of the several advantages of regular meditation. If you have a certain pressing thought in your mind that is distracting you, agree to set it aside with the promise of confronting it later after your meditation session. You must keep the promise of confronting the thought or problem otherwise it will never work in future sessions. The following are tips on how to relax your body and mind:

-Listening to sounds

You do this by zoning out your thoughts and tuning your mind to the sounds in your surrounding environment. This exercise is good in that it allows you to relax and creates awareness as well.

-Awareness of energy in and out your body

You should become aware of the energy inside of you then after a few minutes, focus on the energy that's outside your body and alternate 4 or 5 times. You should do this slowly to feel the energy. The awareness of energy created by this exercise not only enhances your awareness of the environment and other fields but also secures you the ability to absorb and manipulate the energy in the magical workings of meditation. Another benefit of this exercise is to tone your nervous system.

-Be well-rested

Before beginning each session of meditation, make sure that you are well-rested. Meditating while tired does not allow you to accomplish your meditative goals as you will end up falling asleep for the whole session. It is advisable to avoid all the possible distracting physical stimuli unless you are meditating upon a discomfort or pain to strengthen your will.

Note*:* Meditation does not necessarily involve preparing as we've done it above. However, for a beginner, it is important to follow the above process to get you started.

Chapter 3 Effective Mindfulness Meditations

Mindful Breathing

Deep breathing is involved in all of the meditations that are written in this book. It is vital because it helps us calm down, physically, and mentally. Many people, even those who do not practice mindfulness or meditation, use the deep breathing method to help them with panic attacks or experiences of anxiety.

Sit on a chair and with your feet on the floor Or find a place to lie down.
Take a comfortable position. Relax and release all the tension. Gently close your eyes.
Place your hands onto your belly And allow them to rest gently.
Start by observing your breath.

Try not to judge the pace.
Don't rush the process.

Simply observe your breath. Notice your belly rising and falling.

Now take a deep breath through your nose for 5 seconds,

Hold it for 5 seconds

Then breathe out gradually for 7 seconds, and hold for a few seconds.

Breathe in 1...2...3...4...5 Hold 1...2...3...4...5

And release 1...2...3...4...5...6...7

Again, begin filling up your belly with a slow inhalation,

So it starts to feel like a little beach ball or globe.

Imagine a balloon being filled up.

Do not do this roughly or too fast.

Focus on breathing into your stomach and not allowing your shoulders to lift as you inhale.

Breathe out slowly to the count of 7. Try to do this as slowly as possible.

After exhaling, hold for about 2-3 seconds before you inhale into your belly again.

Breathe in expanding your belly,

Hold 1...2...3...4...5,

And release 1...2...3...4...5...6...7.

Breathe in and out this way and observe how your breath has slowed down.

Practice this for around 10 minutes. When you are ready
Gently open your eyes.

Be aware

During this meditation we will focus to be mindful, to be aware of them now.

Find the time and a place where you won't be

disturbed.

Sit or lay down.
Get into a comfortable position. Release all the tension.
Close your eyes.
Now notice your breathing.
Breathe in through the nose to the count of 4, And breathe out more slowly to the count of 6.
Breathe in 1...2...3...4,
And out 1...2...3...4...5...6. Don't force yourself to breathe, just do that as best as you can.
Repeat again.
Breathe in 1...2...3...4,

And exhale slowly 1...2...3...4...5...6.

Focus on the still place between inhaling and exhaling.

If thoughts are coming, visualize them as colored balloons, Separate from you, And let them go.

You are present and aware now,

You are not controlled by your thoughts.

You know that they are simply thoughts,

they do not own you.

You control your thoughts.

You know that you have control of them. Let them go, driven away by the wind.

Become conscious of the heartbeat within you,

Become aware of the rhythm of your breathing.

Breathe in 1...2...3...4

And out 1...2...3...4...5...6.

Become aware of any scent that you can smell.

Notice every detail in the sound you are hearing.

Feel the temperature of the space you are in.

Spend some moment becoming aware of all that is within you and around you. Right now, at this moment...

This is what you need to be mindful. Again, inhale slowly and deeply 1...2...3...4. Now exhale 1...2...3...4...5...6.

(A minute of silence).

Now you are ready to come back to your daily life.

Gently open your eyes.

You can return to this mindfulness guide Whenever you want.

Be present

With this meditation, you are going to experience positive messages And you will be fully present with them.

Begin sitting or lying in a comfortable position.

Relax your head, your arms, your legs.

When you are in a comfortable position

Close your eyes.

Become aware of your breath.

Do nothing.

Just focus on your breath flowing in and out of your nose.

At this moment you are fully present with your breath.

Immerse yourself in this experience.

Staying present with the sensations you are feeling.
Everything is ok.
You are relaxing.
It is a wonderful practice of being mindful.
Breathe normally.
Don't try to control it or change it.
It is perfect.
Just like you are.
There is nothing to change at this moment.
At this moment you are exactly where it needs to be.

It is a beautiful practice.
You are doing a powerful job. Training your mind and your body. You deserve to experience mindfulness.
You deserve the feeling of being in a present moment.

Fully connected with your emotions, with your sensations fully present, fully in the now.

Take a deep breath and,
When you exhale with your nose.
Notice how your body feels.
Notice your emotional state.
You are so peaceful.

You are relaxed.

The best gift to yourself is to be present. You are present with your thoughts and it is just the fact that you exist.

At this moment, the feeling of being present, the feeling of being here now, it is the most beautiful present you give yourself! Take another deep breath and whenever you feel ready. Open your eyes

In the Moment

Position yourself in either a seated or laying down posture.

Allow your hands to rest gently in your lap.
If you are unable to sit comfortably on a meditation cushion, sit then in a chair with both feet on the floor, and a straight spine.

Establish mindfulness of breathing practicing a breath in and a breath out.

The mind can easily turn these breaths into a large thing or distressing task.

This ongoing seamless way of acting, it is important to understand that this is a practice a way of being.

Understand that this practice of being is here and

now.

Create the concept of relaxing or participating mindfully in the fullness of breathing.

Allow your imagination to extend thought time days, weeks, months.

The mind creates a mental image of how things are supposed to be.

Now compare the self-experience with the image of how it should be and how you fall short.

See the feeling of inadequacy, imperfections, and frustrations?

When finding yourself unable to concentrate on the mindfulness of breathing that frustration is blocking the harmony in your breath.

Take a pause and simplify the action of breath. Be aware of the single in-breath, be aware of the single out-breath.

Focus on the immediate and present moment rather than the entirety of the project.

Feel the breath coming into the lunch. Feel the chest raise and the energy flow in.

Exhale letting the stress and frustration leave the body.

When the mind grabs onto an idea, a thought, fear or hope, it gets caught up in these sensations.

The mind can become entangled and caught up in these sensations.

Recognize this and with the out-breath, let go of the feeling of stressfulness.

The heart recognizes these sensations as a burden, causing tension and imbalance.

It is necessary to recognize this and let these feelings go.

Not because "I" should let go but because of the simple quality of mindfulness and wisdom is brought to the experience of grasping.

It is fully known that grasping is hard to sustain. Imagine you are caring for three heavy bags.

At realization the bags are heavy it is difficult to keep ahold of them.

With the natural reaction being to put them down and take a rest.

Asking yourself, "Do I really need all of this extra

baggage?"

The mind works in a similar way you are caring for those stresses, fears, hopes.

Letting go of these with mindfulness is a natural attunement of the mind to present realities.

Inclining a way to free the tension and adjust grasping.

Allowing the mind to let go of that feeling, sound, stress, fantasy, memory the attention settles back on the breathing.

Back into the moment feeling the in-breath and the out-breath.

Notice how this quality of awakened awareness is free from the grasp and the mind is in the present reality.

Feel the heart and now, the reality free of grasping. How does this moment feel?

Feel the peaceful space, a freeing and beautiful state.

Soak in the beauty of this feeling.

The free heart is a quality free of grasping — full of this quality with the mind awake to the present reality.

In these qualities' spaciousness, simplicity, and peacefulness.

Let the effects of grasping be known to themselves and allow the effects of non-grasping to carry their message.

Settle the mind and feel the rhythm of the breath feel the moment.

Feel the naturalness of alertness, the business of the systems of the things carried in the week.

The task was completed and fresh in the body.

The natural echoes of activates of the past week. These ordinary natural effects.

Breathe in and feel re-energized.

Allow the aptitude of patience, forgiveness, regardless of where the mind wanders.

Free the mind from getting caught up with planning, remembering, creating, and time.

Gently notice that these distractions are grasping of the past and future.

Allow yourself to let them go one breath at a time, one moment at a time.

It is constructive not to think of the breaths as something complex or demanding.

They are not a project taking weeks or months.

See the breath as just one exhalation of out-breath and inhalation of in-breath.

Feel the fulfillment of mindfulness of breathing.

Pay only attention to the breath, exhale… no need to complicate.

Inhale… just breathing. No need to complicate or uncomplicated.

Develop a response mode of noticing when distracting feelings, or tensions blossom.

Then release those feelings with the out-breath.

Re-centering the attention to being aware. Freeing the mind of grasping.

The mind with the open quality of alertness, peace, non-personal.

Self-centering habits may move in — "I've got some idea…" "I had it all under control…" "I've lost it."

Notice these mental self-created habits thinking in the mind creating complications.

Let them out-breath funnel them away releasing tension and stress.

The natural relinquishing releasing quality of the out-breath.

Allow the in-breath to fill the space with energization and invigorating quality.

Through inspired breathing the mind brightens, livens, brings life to the body and heals.

Qualities of peacefulness, calmness, awareness strengthen the mind.

The fixation of attention to breathing is no longer necessary as breathing now serves as an anchor to help guide the attention.

Mindful Relaxation

Start by sitting down comfortably.
If you are sitting on a cushion, cross your legs in front of you.

In case you are sitting on a chair, lay your feet on the floor.

After finding the right posture, straighten your upper body.

Try to soften your gaze so that you don't strain too much.
Drop your chin and look downward gently.
It is inevitable that your mind will start wandering off during the meditation practice.

Don't panic or try to block thoughts from trickling in.
Moreover, be gentle with your mind when it starts wandering.

Your mind may start wandering constantly and rather than fighting the thoughts, observe them without reaction.

Focus on how the thoughts unfold and then focus on your breath.

Become aware of your breath.
Don't rush the process.
Just notice the rhythm of your breathing.
Now, take a few deep breaths.
Inhale deeply through your nose, exhale slowly through your mouth. Again, breathe in slowly,

Then gradually exhale.
Notice your breathing pattern and focus on the physical sensation.

Breathe in… and exhale.
Allow your body to relax.

Relax your muscles by letting loose your whole body.

Take your awareness to the top of your head.
Do you feel the muscles there?
Now, relax the top, back, and sides of your head.
Soften the forehead.
Move to the eyebrows and soften them.
Feel your eyes and soften the muscles at the back of your eyes.

Soften your cheeks and ears.
Relax the muscles on your jaw.
These must be tensed.
Let them relax completely.
Feel your tongue and relax it.
Relax your lips.
Drop to your throat.
Does it feel dry on the inside?

Allow the muscles around it to soften and relax it.

Listen to the back of your neck.
Do you feel the stiffness around it?
Now relax your neck gently.
Take your awareness to your shoulders and relax them.

Take your focus to your arms and hands.
Feel them getting limb - then relax them.
Feel all your ten fingers.
Relax each finger and thumb one by one.
Relax your palms.
Drop to your chest and relax it.
Soften its muscles and feel them letting go.
Move to your stomach and back.
Relax the muscles in your whole midsection.
Relax your back from the shoulders going down to your buttocks.

Can you feel your thighs?
Notice how strong your thighs are.
Take your awareness to the right thigh and relax it.
Relax your right knee down to the right ankle and the whole foot including the toes.

Become aware of your left thigh.
Let it loose and relax.

Feel your left knee down to your left ankle and relax the whole of it and don't leave the foot and the toes.

Listen to your whole body and listen to any area that you can feel tension lodged there.

Scan your whole body as you relax the tensed areas.

Feel your whole body totally relaxed.
Fully relaxed.
It's time to come back.
Stabilize your breath.

Become aware of your whole body and feel it waking up.

Feel all your body parts moving gently.
Slowly lift your gaze.

Mindfulness Meditation to Find Calm

This meditation can reduce stressful situations in your everyday life, or just whenever you want to feel calm. To begin, sit on a chair with your feet on the floor, or lay down on a comfortable bed.
Inhale through your nose to the count of 4, exhale through your mouth to the count of 3. Do that 3 times:

Inhale 1...2...3...4,
And exhale 1...2...3.
Inhale 1...2...3...4,
And exhale 1...2...3.

Inhale 1...2...3...4,
And exhale 1...2...3.
Imagine a white light enters through you from your feet.

It is a warm light.
Feel it into each muscle,
Into every fiber of your body.
You feel this warm light in your legs,
You feel it in your knees,
Like you are in a warm bath.
Let it flow into your body.
Any tension in your muscles is leaving your body.
Now inhale through your nose to the count of 4,
And exhale through your mouth to the count of 3.
Do that 3 times:
Inhale 1...2...3...4,
And exhale 1...2...3.

Inhale 1...2...3...4,
And exhale 1...2...3.
Inhale 1...2...3...4,

And exhale 1...2...3.

Feel this warm light in your upper body. Let it flow into your chest, into your throat. Feel it in your face. It illuminates your face like sunlight.

Any tension in your head and in your mind is leaving.

You are feeling calm and confident.

Say to yourself:
- I AM CALM
- I AM CONFIDENT
- I AM PEACEFUL

Now imagine the light flowing out of you.

Taking away all your tensions.

Now the light is surrounding you like a protective aura.

Take a deep breath...

Inhale 1...2...3...4,

And exhale 1...2...3.

You are feeling calm and confident.

Repeat to yourself:
- I AM CALM
- I AM CONFIDENT
- I AM PEACEFUL

Feel the peace and the warmth of the light resting in you.

The light is there for you.
Whenever you need to feel calm.

Mindful Morning Meditation

Below is a guided mindfulness meditation that you can practice in the morning.

This session will turn your day into a mindful one.

Please find a place that you can settle in where no one will disturb you.

You may sit on the floor or in a chair.
If you are on the floor, let your feet be flat on it.
If you are sitting on a chair, let your legs rest on a cushion.

You can also take a walk in the park.
It doesn't matter where you choose to be as long as you are comfortable.
Please be reminded that it is okay to have thoughts during this mediation.

When they come, relax, and allow them in.
Don't try to fight them.

Settle in this guided meditation and stick with it to the end.

Close your eyes completely or halfway.
Direct your awareness to your breath.
Notice as your body moves when you inhale and exhale.

Breathe in and feel the air move from your nose to your body.

Feel it fill your lungs and chest.
Now release slowly.
Breathe in till you cannot inhale anymore and pause.

Feel your body becoming limb. Now
breathe out slowly to the end. Notice
the silence around.
You might notice your thought wandering.
It is okay.
It is alright if you find yourself taking your thought elsewhere.

Cut yourself some slack and gently bring them back to the meditation.

Do not judge yourself. Continue to breathe in and out

as you bring your awareness to the movements in your chest.

Notice how your chest is moving up and down as you inhale and exhale.
Breathe in and pause as you reach the end of the inhale.

Exhale slowly as you listen to the silence around you.

Now take three fake yawns until you get a real one.
Yawn!
Yawn!
Yawn!
Yaaaaaawwwn!
Perfect, there you had a real yawn.
Did you notice what the yawn did to your breathing?

Your breathing stabilized and took back its original rhythm.

Now, think of the sun and its bright yellow rays.
Think of its warmth infusing in your body.
Let the rays surround your whole body and loosen it.

Breathe in and exhale slowly.

Feel the sun rays waking your whole body.
Breathe in and send oxygen to your whole body, then exhale.
Feel every limb getting ready for the day.
Feel every cell expanding with the expectations of the day.

Breathe in, breathe out gently.
Allow the sun to shine rays of energy to your whole body.

Feel as your body is powering up from the oxygen you are breathing.

Feel it energizing from the sun rays.

Take a deep breath that penetrates your heart.
Let the golden rays energize your heart center.
Allow your heart to get ready for a new day.
Gently direct your attention to your breathing.
Focus on your breath for the next few minutes.
(Pause)
Don't shy away from your thoughts.
They are okay.
Don't condemn yourself but make sure they don't take you away from the meditation.

If they do, it is still okay; concentrate on your breathing, and you will be back on the meditation.

If you had closed your eyes halfway at the beginning of the meditation, slowly allow them to close.

It is important to come out of this process slowly.
Keep concentrating on your breath.
Feel the air as it goes through your nostrils to your whole body and then leaves.

Feel the movement of your chest.
You can move your arms gently.
Wiggle your toes and fingers.
Do you feel ready to face the day?
Now open your eyes slowly but maintain your focus inward.

Are your eyes fully open?
Welcome back and get ready to have a mindful day.
You may now begin your blessed day.

Mindful Visualization

If the images suggested in this book are not working for you, you are welcome to try other methods of visualization that connects more directly with who you are. While most meditations will suggest that you visualize a flower or something in nature that is relaxing, you may want to think of a more personal image that resonates with you in your life. You may want to think of a pet that you love, running around in the field, and playing happily. Or perhaps it is the fall of rain or snow. Whatever the image may be, make sure that it is a relaxing one, not one that stimulates any negative feelings or sensations. It is best not to think of other people, as other people tend to come with their subconscious associations that we are not yet aware of.

To prepare for this meditation, which you will be feeling very relaxed,

Find a quiet place where you won't be disturbed.
Make sure you are sitting comfortably on a soft chair

Or laying down on a comfortable bed.
Now close your eyes.
Breathe in deeply.
Exhale releasing any tension you may be feeling
Through your breath.
Take another deep breath now.

Exhale slowly.

Feel any tension leaving your body.
Now imagine that you are sitting on a quiet beach, you can see the blue ocean, you can hear the waves. Observe the sea for a time. Observe its movement, Smell the scent of the sea.
Let it enter your nose and spread through your body.

Now breathe in deeply and breathe out releasing any tension. You feel peace in your body
And in your mind...
You are feeling so relaxed.
You follow the flow of the ocean,
And you are feeling so calm and peaceful.

Enjoy being here in this quiet place.
Now breathe in deeply,
And breathe out releasing any tension from your body.

(1-minute silence)
When you are ready to come back to your daily routine,

Open your eyes.
Now... you feel so relaxed and peaceful.
Now you are ready for your everyday life.

Refreshing Mind & Body

This is a walking meditation; this meditation is best performed outdoors but can also be experienced inside (for example in the gym). Ensure you are wearing comfortable clothes and shoes as you prepare for this meditation.

With walking meditation, we bring the mind, breath, and body to harmony.

Feel free to fold your hands and carry them at the waist, or to allow them to set to the sides of the body.

Relax the shoulders, the face, while maintaining that the spine is straight.

Feel the flow of energy through the spine, your inner life-force.

Now begin taking the first step, inhale and gently step with the left foot.

As the foot touches the ground being mindful of the breath, where is the breath?

You very well still could be inhaling, or you may have moved to exhale.

Neither is right or wrong.

Just be aware of your breath as you take these first steps.

Now let us focus on the in-breath with the first step and the out-breath as the next step.

Feel the foot solidly against the ground the breath flowing from the body.

On the next in-breath, step with the right foot.

As you settle into the patter of walking allow the mind to pay attention to the sensations of the floor.

The heal meeting the ground with each step. Feel as the heal moves to the toe then forward. Now let's focus the step with the breath.

Inhaling as we raise the foot and the foot rises from the ground.

As the, heal makes contact with the floor, the ball of the foot, then the toes.

Feel each sensation as the breath completes take pause.

Practice for the next few steps one breath—one step.

With slowly with awareness of each movement. On the next in-breath, step with the right foot.

Inhaling as we raise the foot and the foot rises from the ground.

As the foot makes contact with the floor, the ball of the foot, then the toes.

Feel each sensation as the breath completes take pause.

Now repeat this phrase:

- One breath—One step
- One breath—One step
- One breath—One step

Feel the refreshing awaking as you continue walking.

Focusing only on one breath, one step.

Attune your body to the sensation that is each step or walking.

Be mindful of this as you step.

Aware of the feeling of your body becoming at peace.

Notice how your body begins to send sensations to the mind's sensations of energy.

Accept that you will listen to the body and acknowledge each step.

Notice as you now that the path in front of you is more than a rushed experience.

Feel your body no longer mindless walking.

Through this practice notice the slowing down and appreciation for each step before you.

Acknowledge the heightened awareness of the body's need to maintain overall health.

Feel yourself becoming open welcoming to enjoy the walk.

Resolve that in the next walk you will become more and more aware and mindful with each step.

One step at a time.

Eating With Meaning

Position yourself in a comfortable seated posture at a table or on a bench.
With your meal in front of you.
Settle the body into your seat with a mindful posture maintain a straight back.
Sitting back in your seat ready to nourish the body.
Open your mind to the acceptance that the way you eat is important.

That through mindful eating, you will eat with purpose.

Feel the heightened awareness in this very moment.

Engage your body with the idea of hunger.

Not the mindless act of putting food into your mouth to sustain your body.

Be aware that the food is the fuel for your body.

That filling your body with premium food will allow it to perform at a heightened level.

Engage your body to decipher between clues of hunger and boredom.

Focus your body that food is not the answer to deal with experiences of stress or guilt.

Accept that food is only fuel for the body.

That only premium fuel entering into the body will provide heightened experience.

Feel the weight of your body, not a heaviness or lightness just the pull of gravity holding you gently to the earth.

Feel the sensations of the skin, the warmth or coolness of the body.

Allow yourself to feel sensory pains or aches in the body.

Accept all these sensations and allow yourself to be

open to being at this moment.

You hear, and now with this nourishment, this food.

Immerse yourself in the aroma and visual appeal of the food.

Welcome the savory sensations that come from your meal, the scent, the texture.

As you prepare for the first bite be mindful as you lift your hand or utensil.

Raising the hand, lifting the arm, gently placing the food into the mouth.

Notice the aroma, the texture of the bit.

Notice as it got closer your mouth beginning to salivate.

Be aware of all the sensations as these occur and note them in your mind.

Turn your focus now to chewing the food.

Marking that the point of concentration is now the act of chewing.

Similarly, to the realizing of each in-breath and out-breath.

Realize that with chewing it is the motion of the mouth.

Commit to chewing each bit 20 times. This may vary

by food consistency or type.

Allow that number of chews to be the anchor for your focus.

Only chew for that magic number.

Do not think ahead to the next bit.

Do not prepare to move the fork around on your plate.

Be only at that moment with your food chewing.

As you feel the texture within your mouth allows your tongue to experience the explosion of taste, your nose to breathe in the aroma, your eyes full of wonder and excitement as the bite enters your mouth.

As you begin to chew focus only on the act of chewing.

Those 20 magical chews, knowing that with mindful eating you are treating your body as a temple.

Place the next bit in your welcoming mouth.

Allowing the mouth to experience the texture and turning back to chewing.

All along having an open and welcoming position to what may arise or not while eating.

More than just the food in front of you may arise within the mind you may feel sensations within the body.

Allow those sensations to form and then fall away.

You may find yourself lost in a feeling or thought, be

aware that it is simply just a feeling or thought.

Allow it to rise and fall away without judgment.

Do not worry if these feelings are worthy or unworthy of attention.

Know that at this moment you are in a place where everything is accepted.

Allowing thoughts to simply be.

Attune your body to the sensation that is hunger or fullness.

Be mindful of this as you chew.

Aware of the feeling of your body becoming full.

Notice how your body begins to send sensations to the mind of the level of fullness.

Accept that you will listen to the body and acknowledge the fullness.

Notice as you now that the food in front of you is more than a rushed experience.

Feel your body no longer mindless shoveling bite after bite into the mouth.

Gorged and deaf to the body's needs and wants.

Through this practice notice the slowing down and appreciation for the food before you.

Acknowledge the heightened awareness of the body's need to maintain overall health.

Accept that food is fuel, not a replacement for emotion.
Feel open, welcoming to enjoy the meal.
Resolve that with the next meal you will become more and more aware and mindful with each bite, and chew.

Chapter 4 The Light Warrior Meditation

This third meditation combines the Body Scan meditation and the Meditation of the Sun, bringing you a deep sense of relaxing and relieving you from anxiety.

I have used this technique during the most difficult periods of my life and it has helped me to come up on top of things. That is why it has a special place in my heart and why I decided to share it in this book. I really want everyone to benefit from it.

First, we will start the meditation with a deep body scan, as shown in the very first technique of the book. We will take our time to go through it properly, as it will be our grounding phase and it plays an important role in the entire practice.

Secondly, we will spend some time performing the liquid sunlight exercise, as it will give us the ability to melt anxiety and stress away from our bodies.

Finally, we will direct our attention to loving and kind thoughts, which will be our priming for the rest of the day. Focusing on the good always attracts positive in our life, that is why the Light Warrior goes through life with good vibes and intentions: he knows the world is a mirror and will give him back what he brings to the world.

Let's get started!

Find a comfortable, relaxed, and balanced position. Give yourself permission to be completely present for yourself, and let your body and mind calm down until they become soft and relaxed.

Breathe in, feel relaxed...
breathe out, feel calm.

Breathe in, feel relaxed...
breathe out, feel calm.

Breathe in, feel relaxed...
breathe out, feel calm.

Breathe in, feel relaxed...
breathe out, feel calm.

Allow the mind to distance itself from all thoughts and orientate awareness on your breath. Breathe naturally and do not force a specific rhythm. Let your breath come and go.

Carefully, now, drive your attention from the breath to the space in which you are.

Feel the energy and atmosphere of this space as it permeates all of your being. Notice the noises in the background. Maybe there is a clock ticking, maybe there are cars passing just outside your windows. Whatever you feel it is fine, let your attention rest on the external.

Breathe in, feel relaxed...
breathe out, feel calm.

Breathe in, feel relaxed...
breathe out, feel calm.

Breathe in, feel relaxed...
breathe out, feel calm.

Breathe in, feel relaxed...

breathe out, feel calm.

Now bring the attention back to the breath. Take your time and you will naturally reach a place of warmth and ease. Stay in this state where you feel your body and mind completely calm, relaxed, and full of peace for a few minutes, without letting go the focus on your breath.

Breathe in, feel relaxed...
breathe out, feel calm.

Breathe in, feel relaxed...
breathe out, feel calm.

Breathe in, feel relaxed...
breathe out, feel calm.

Breathe in, feel relaxed...
breathe out, feel calm.

Breathe in, feel relaxed...
breathe out, feel calm.

Breathe in, feel relaxed...

breathe out, feel calm.

Breathe in, feel relaxed...
breathe out, feel calm.

Breathe in, feel relaxed...
breathe out, feel calm.

Now, begin to scan your body from the bottom of your toes up to the top of your head. Do this slowly and stop on each part of your body to listen to what it has to tell you. If you feel contracted in aspecific area, keep the attention on that part for as long as you feel it relaxing. It is important that you do not force this process, just keep breathing and you will feel your body getting more and more relaxed.

Begin from your big toes, how do they feel today? Have you ever asked yourself this question? Painta clear picture of them inside your head, as you slowly shift your attention to your ankles.

During this practice, each joint is a crucial point where anxiety can infiltrate itself. If you find a part of your body that feels tight, you can softly massage it with your hands until you feel it completely relaxed.

Breathe in, feel relaxed...
breathe out, feel calm.

Breathe in, feel relaxed...
breathe out, feel calm.

Breathe in, feel relaxed…
breathe out, feel calm.

Breathe in, feel relaxed…
breathe out, feel calm.

Reach your knees and feel them. How are your knees today? Maybe they are sore because you have been standing all day or made an effort yesterday. Maybe they are relaxed and strong. Whatever you feel, it is okay. Moving up your quadriceps, reach your pelvic floor and genital area.

This is an extremely crucial zone of your body when it comes to anxiety and stress, as a lot of energy is drawn down to it by your neuromuscular system. Spend a few minutes on your pelvic, before moving upwards. I will give you the time you need.

Breathe in, feel relaxed…
breathe out, feel calm.

Breathe in, feel relaxed…
breathe out, feel calm.

Breathe in, feel relaxed…
breathe out, feel calm.

Breathe in, feel relaxed...
breathe out, feel calm.

Breathe in, feel relaxed...
breathe out, feel calm.

Breathe in, feel relaxed...
breathe out, feel calm.

Breathe in, feel relaxed...
breathe out, feel calm.

Breathe in, feel relaxed...
breathe out, feel calm.

Breathe in, feel relaxed...
breathe out, feel calm.

Breathe in, feel relaxed...
breathe out, feel calm.

Breathe in, feel relaxed...
breathe out, feel calm.

Breathe in, feel relaxed...
breathe out, feel calm.

Keep going up, reaching your chest and your shoulders. This is where a lot of tension can be usually found, so take your time in this area. If you feel a bit stiff, do not hesitate to move your arms, until they reach a comfortable position. Feel your lungs and heart, still beating strong, even if you had a rough day or are facing issues at the moment.

The heart keeps beating, the lungs keep breathing. Breathe in, feel relaxed...

breathe out, feel calm.

Breathe in, feel relaxed...
breathe out, feel calm.

Breathe in, feel relaxed...
breathe out, feel calm.

Breathe in, feel relaxed...
breathe out, feel calm.

Breathe in, feel relaxed...
breathe out, feel calm.

Breathe in, feel relaxed...
breathe out, feel calm.

Breathe in, feel relaxed...
breathe out, feel calm.

Breathe in, feel relaxed...
breathe out, feel calm.

And finally, you reach your head. Keep breathing into your head and feel the air slowly filling every empty space of your head.

How does the air feel? Is it cold or warm? What does it smell like? Do you like it? Those are all simple questions that we forget to ask ourself during the day, but that can help us ground ourself back into our body.

Breathe in, feel relaxed...
breathe out, feel calm.

Breathe in, feel relaxed...
breathe out, feel calm.

Breathe in, feel relaxed...
breathe out, feel calm.

Breathe in, feel relaxed...
breathe out, feel calm.
Stay in this beautiful space for as long as you want, you deserve it.

Breathe in, feel relaxed...
breathe out, feel calm.

Breathe in, feel relaxed...
breathe out, feel calm.
Breathe in, feel relaxed...
breathe out, feel calm.
Breathe in, feel relaxed...
breathe out, feel calm.
Breathe in, feel relaxed...
breathe out, feel calm.
Breathe in, feel relaxed...
breathe out, feel calm.
Breathe in, feel relaxed...
breathe out, feel calm.
Breathe in, feel relaxed...
breathe out, feel calm.
Breathe in, feel relaxed...
breathe out, feel calm.
Breathe in, feel relaxed...
breathe out, feel calm.
Breathe in, feel relaxed...
breathe out, feel calm.
Breathe in, feel relaxed...
breathe out, feel calm.

Breathe in, feel relaxed...
breathe out, feel calm.

Breathe in, feel relaxed...
breathe out, feel calm.
Breathe in, feel relaxed...
breathe out, feel calm.
Breathe in, feel relaxed...
breathe out, feel calm.

Now bring the attention back to the body and start feeling your arms and legs once again. You can close your hands or move your fingers, just to take control of the space around you.

Please, keep the eyes closed for now and enjoy the beautiful moment you are living. You have given yourself the time to feel better and that is absolutely incredible.

Breathe in, feel relaxed...
breathe out, feel calm.

Breathe in, feel relaxed...
breathe out, feel calm.

Breathe in, feel relaxed...
breathe out, feel calm.

Breathe in, feel relaxed...
breathe out, feel calm.

In your time, try to imagine a sphere of liquid sunlight just a few inches above your head. Imagining a small sun can be beneficial during this part, as it helps your mind and body to adapt to this new entity.

With every breath now, feel the liquid sunlight coming down into your head and through your spine, reaching the bottom of your feet through your pelvic floor and legs. Your body is getting filled with this warm and soft light. Can you feel it?

If you are struggling, it is fine, do not force it too much. It will get better over time.

Breathe in, feel relaxed...
breathe out, feel calm.

Breathe in, feel relaxed...
breathe out, feel calm.

Breathe in, feel relaxed...
breathe out, feel calm.

Breathe in, feel relaxed...
breathe out, feel calm.

Breathe in, feel relaxed...
breathe out, feel calm.

Breathe in, feel relaxed...
breathe out, feel calm.

Breathe in, feel relaxed...

breathe out, feel calm.

Breathe in, feel relaxed...
breathe out, feel calm.

The liquid sunlight is filling every inch of your body and is taking away all the anxiety and the stress of the day. Keep breathing, I will give you a few more minutes to stay in this state as the liquid sunlight is purifying your body and soul.

Breathe in, feel relaxed...
breathe out, feel calm.

Breathe in, feel relaxed...
breathe out, feel calm.

Breathe in, feel relaxed...
breathe out, feel calm.

Breathe in, feel relaxed...
breathe out, feel calm.

Breathe in, feel relaxed...
breathe out, feel calm.

Breathe in, feel relaxed...
breathe out, feel calm.

Breathe in, feel relaxed...
breathe out, feel calm.

Breathe in, feel relaxed...
breathe out, feel calm.

Breathe in, feel relaxed...
breathe out, feel calm.

Breathe in, feel relaxed...
breathe out, feel calm.

Breathe in, feel relaxed...
breathe out, feel calm.

Breathe in, feel relaxed...
breathe out, feel calm.

Breathe in, feel relaxed...
breathe out, feel calm.

Breathe in, feel relaxed...
breathe out, feel calm.

Breathe in, feel relaxed…
breathe out, feel calm.

Breathe in, feel relaxed…
breathe out, feel calm.
As the light comes down your body, feel your body being filled not only with the warm liquid, but with positive and loving thoughts as well.

Focus your attention on everything good that is going on in the world. The fact that you are alive and breathing is a miracle in itself, so acknowledge it inside your mind. Picture something that makes you happy and that resembles positive energy in your life.

Personally, I like to picture a beautiful white flower, but you can choose whatever fits your soul the best. Just paint it in your mind and breathe into it.

Breathe in, feel relaxed…
breathe out, feel calm.

Breathe in, feel relaxed…
breathe out, feel calm.

Breathe in, feel relaxed…
breathe out, feel calm.

Breathe in, feel relaxed...
breathe out, feel calm.
Having a clear image is key, as it will allow you to take it with you during the rest of the entire day. So, I will give you all the time you need.

Breathe in, feel relaxed...
breathe out, feel calm.

Breathe in, feel relaxed...
breathe out, feel calm.

Breathe in, feel relaxed...
breathe out, feel calm.

Breathe in, feel relaxed...
breathe out, feel calm.

Breathe in, feel relaxed...
breathe out, feel calm.

Breathe in, feel relaxed...
breathe out, feel calm.

Breathe in, feel relaxed...
breathe out, feel calm.

Breathe in, feel relaxed...
breathe out, feel calm.

Breathe in, feel relaxed...
breathe out, feel calm.

Breathe in, feel relaxed...
breathe out, feel calm.

Breathe in, feel relaxed...
breathe out, feel calm.

Breathe in, feel relaxed...
breathe out, feel calm.

Now bring the attention back to the body and start feeling your arms and legs once again. You can close your hands or move your fingers, just to take control of the space around you.

Please, keep the eyes closed for now and enjoy the beautiful moment you are living. You have given yourself the time to feel better and that is absolutely incredible.

Breathe in, feel relaxed...
breathe out, feel calm.

Breathe in, feel relaxed...
breathe out, feel calm.

Breathe in, feel relaxed...
breathe out, feel calm.

Breathe in, feel relaxed...
breathe out, feel calm.
Now become aware of the environment around you once again. Feel the different sounds, the temperature of the room you are in, and once you are ready, open the eyes again.

Chapter 5 The Safe Place Meditation

This meditation is perfect for defeating anxiety and getting in a quieter and more convenient space of mind.

It originates from the ancient Eastern culture and it was used by monks during their initiation period, where they had to face extremely hard circumstances. Nowadays, it is often practiced by endurance athletes, that experience prolonged pain and suffering during training and races.

Courtney Dauwalter, a famous ultra runner and winner of the 2018 edition of Moab 240, 240 miles running race, reported multiple times how she used this technique to go through the most difficult moments of the event.

To give you a quick insight into what we are going to do during the meditation, here is a small recap of the main steps of the practice. After focusing on ourselves and entering a profound space of relaxation, we will picture in our mind a place that reminds us of a beautiful and peaceful moment we have experienced in the past.

That is everything there is to know to approach the practice with enough background information to get the most out of it.
So, let's get started!
Find a comfortable, relaxed, and balanced position. Give yourself permission to be completely present for yourself, and let your body and mind calm down until they become soft and relaxed.

Breathe in, feel relaxed...
breathe out, feel calm.

Breathe in, feel relaxed...
breathe out, feel calm.

Breathe in, feel relaxed...
breathe out, feel calm.

Breathe in, feel relaxed...
breathe out, feel calm.

Allow the mind to distance itself from all thoughts and orientate awareness on your breath. Breathe naturally and do not force a specific rhythm. Let your breath come and go.

Carefully, now, drive your attention from the breath to the space in which you are.

Feel the energy and atmosphere of this space as it permeates all of your being. Notice the noises in the background. Maybe there is a clock ticking, maybe cars are passing just outside your windows. Whatever you feel it is fine, let your attention rest on the external.

Breathe in, feel relaxed...
breathe out, feel calm.

Breathe in, feel relaxed...
breathe out, feel calm.

Breathe in, feel relaxed...
breathe out, feel calm.

Breathe in, feel relaxed...

breathe out, feel calm.

Now bring the attention back to the breath.
Take your time and you will naturally reach a place of warmth and ease.

There is nothing to do here, nothing to think or to worry about. Just rest your attention on the breath, following each inhalation and exhalation with curiosity, falling into the rhythm of your very body.

If you want, you can place your hands on your belly. This will help you enter in connection with the natural movement of the air entering through your nose and exciting trough the mouth.

Breathe in, feel relaxed...
breathe out, feel calm.

Breathe in, feel relaxed...
breathe out, feel calm.

Breathe in, feel relaxed...
breathe out, feel calm.

Breathe in, feel relaxed...
breathe out, feel calm.

Breathe in, feel relaxed...
breathe out, feel calm.

Breathe in, feel relaxed...
breathe out, feel calm.

Breathe in, feel relaxed...

breathe out, feel calm.

Breathe in, feel relaxed…
breathe out, feel calm.
I will give you a few more minutes to get into this zone, as we will then begin the actual practice.

Breathe in, feel relaxed…
breathe out, feel calm.

Breathe in, feel relaxed…
breathe out, feel calm.

Breathe in, feel relaxed…

breathe out, feel calm.

Breathe in, feel relaxed…
breathe out, feel calm.

Breathe in, feel relaxed…
breathe out, feel calm.

Breathe in, feel relaxed…
breathe out, feel calm.

Breathe in, feel relaxed…
breathe out, feel calm.

Breathe in, feel relaxed…
breathe out, feel calm.

Breathe in, feel relaxed...
breathe out, feel calm.

Breathe in, feel relaxed...
breathe out, feel calm.

Breathe in, feel relaxed...
breathe out, feel calm.

Breathe in, feel relaxed...
breathe out, feel calm.

Breathe in, feel relaxed...
breathe out, feel calm.

Breathe in, feel relaxed...
breathe out, feel calm.

Breathe in, feel relaxed...
breathe out, feel calm.

Now start thinking about a moment in the past where you felt incredibly good and safe. Do not rush the process, let the memory come to your mind in a natural way. This is extremely important because remember: in meditation, there is nothing to do, everything comes naturally and arises from within.

Breathe in, feel relaxed...
breathe out, feel calm.

Breathe in, feel relaxed...

breathe out, feel calm.

Breathe in, feel relaxed...

breathe out, feel calm.

If the memory has come to your mind, ask yourself how the location was. Was it in nature? Maybe at home? Just think about it and picture it inside your mind.

Breathe in, feel relaxed...

breathe out, feel calm.

Breathe in, feel relaxed...

breathe out, feel calm.

Breathe in, feel relaxed...

breathe out, feel calm.

After you have got a general idea, try to go a bit deeper and picture a bit more details of the scene. Figure out the sounds, the smells, and the feelings that the place is providing for you. There is no right or wrong way to do this, just try to get as many details as possible, really painting a beautiful and complete picture of the place inside your mind.

Breathe in, feel relaxed...

breathe out, feel calm.

Breathe in, feel relaxed...

breathe out, feel calm.

Breathe in, feel relaxed...

breathe out, feel calm.

Breathe in, feel relaxed...

breathe out, feel calm.

Breathe in, feel relaxed...

breathe out, feel calm.

Breathe in, feel relaxed...
breathe out, feel calm.

Breathe in, feel relaxed...
breathe out, feel calm.

Breathe in, feel relaxed.
breathe out, feel calm.

Focus on the light and the background noise, as getting in touch with the smaller details can help a lot in crafting a complete image.

Breathe in, feel relaxed...
breathe out, feel calm.

Breathe in, feel relaxed...
breathe out, feel calm.

Breathe in, feel relaxed…
breathe out, feel calm.

Breathe in, feel relaxed…
breathe out, feel calm.

Breathe in, feel relaxed…
breathe out, feel calm.

Breathe in, feel relaxed…
breathe out, feel calm.

Breathe in, feel relaxed…
breathe out, feel calm.

Breathe in, feel relaxed…
breathe out, feel calm.

Now that you have the picture clear in your head, it is time to start living in this safe place. Enter the picture with your mind and imagine as if you were there for real. The mind cannot tell the difference between a "fake" or "real" experience, so it does not matter that you are not there physically. If you can imagine being there, you are there.

I know that this is going on a bit of a philosophical path, but you will get a full understanding once you have experienced the entire practice.

Breathe in, feel relaxed...
breathe out, feel calm.

Breathe in, feel relaxed...

breathe out, feel calm.

Breathe in, feel relaxed...
breathe out, feel calm.

Breathe in, feel relaxed...
breathe out, feel calm.

Breathe in, feel relaxed...
breathe out, feel calm.

Breathe in, feel relaxed...
breathe out, feel calm.

Breathe in, feel relaxed...
breathe out, feel calm.

Breathe in, feel relaxed...
breathe out, feel calm.

With every breath, try to get a little deeper and feel a little more inside your safe space. This is a space that is completely yours and that does not hold any judgment at all. You can do whatever you want here, as there are no physical limits, no laws, no rules to follow. In this safe space, reality bends under your control and you are the master of everything, while still being a visitor of the space.

Breathe in, feel relaxed...
breathe out, feel calm.

Breathe in, feel relaxed...
breathe out, feel calm.

Breathe in, feel relaxed...
breathe out, feel calm.

Breathe in, feel relaxed...
breathe out, feel calm.

Breathe in, feel relaxed...
breathe out, feel calm.

Breathe in, feel relaxed...
breathe out, feel calm.

Breathe in, feel relaxed...
breathe out, feel calm.

Breathe in, feel relaxed...
breathe out, feel calm.

I will give you a few minutes to experience the safety of this space by yourself. Let your mind free, as it has nothing to worry about.

Breathe in, feel relaxed...
breathe out, feel calm.

Breathe in, feel relaxed...
breathe out, feel calm.

Breathe in, feel relaxed...
breathe out, feel calm.

Breathe in, feel relaxed...
breathe out, feel calm.

Breathe in, feel relaxed...
breathe out, feel calm.

Breathe in, feel relaxed...
breathe out, feel calm.

Breathe in, feel relaxed...
breathe out, feel calm.

Breathe in, feel relaxed...
breathe out, feel calm.

Breathe in, feel relaxed...
breathe out, feel calm.

Breathe in, feel relaxed...
breathe out, feel calm.

Breathe in, feel relaxed...
breathe out, feel calm.

Breathe in, feel relaxed...
breathe out, feel calm.

Breathe in, feel relaxed...
breathe out, feel calm.

Breathe in, feel relaxed...
breathe out, feel calm.

Breathe in, feel relaxed...

breathe out, feel calm.

Breathe in, feel relaxed...
breathe out, feel calm.

Breathe in, feel relaxed...
breathe out, feel calm.

Breathe in, feel relaxed...
breathe out, feel calm.

Breathe in, feel relaxed...
breathe out, feel calm.

Breathe in, feel relaxed...
breathe out, feel calm.

Breathe in, feel relaxed...
breathe out, feel calm.

Breathe in, feel relaxed...
breathe out, feel calm.

Breathe in, feel relaxed...
breathe out, feel calm.

Breathe in, feel relaxed...
breathe out, feel calm.

And now that we are approaching the end of the practice, just know that you can enter this space whenever you desire. It will always be there for you; it will not go away. Once you discover this state of mind, or space, inside of you, you know that every time you feel anxious or worried, you can go back to this sensation and melt everything away.

Feel the freedom, as freedom is the cure.
Breathe in, feel relaxed...
breathe out, feel calm.
Breathe in, feel relaxed...
breathe out, feel calm.
Breathe in, feel relaxed...
breathe out, feel calm.

Breathe in, feel relaxed...
breathe out, feel calm.
Breathe in, feel relaxed...
breathe out, feel calm.
Breathe in, feel relaxed...
breathe out, feel calm.
Breathe in, feel relaxed...
breathe out, feel calm.
Breathe in, feel relaxed...
breathe out, feel calm.
Now bring the attention back to the body and start feeling your arms and legs once again. You can close your hands or move your fingers, just to take control of the space around you.

Please, keep the eyes closed for now and enjoy the beautiful moment you are living. You have given yourself the time to feel better and that is incredible.

Breathe in, feel relaxed...
breathe out, feel calm.

Breathe in, feel relaxed...
breathe out, feel calm.

Breathe in, feel relaxed...
breathe out, feel calm.

Breathe in, feel relaxed...
breathe out, feel calm.

Now become aware of the environment around you once again. Feel the different sounds, the temperature of the room you are in, and once you are ready, open the eyes again.

Chapter 6 Changing Maladaptive Thinking With CBT

Changing maladaptive thinking is an extension of psychology and one of its core principles. In this section, we are going to discuss mainstream cognitive therapy.

Essentially, this therapy holds that changes in maladaptive thinking will lead to changes in behavior. While this is true on the surface, there are other important factors to consider that are part of why CBT is much more effective than simple cognitive therapy.

Cognitive therapy attacks cognitive distortions that are causing maladaptive behavior in a person's daily life. For example, the belief that everything a person does will fail is a cognitive distortion and needs to be challenged by the therapist.

Cognitive distortions and challenging the thinking, however, are only the beginning of the process. The reason why CBT is so effective is that the main goal of CBT as we will see is all-inclusive and requires interaction and change by the patient.

The Main Goal of CBT

Cognitive distortions lead us into the importance of a complete therapy that takes into consideration the final goal of adaptive behavior, as well as the thoughts and feelings of the patient who seeks to normalize their behavior and interact successfully with society again.

This is what separates basic cognitive therapy from CBT; the ability to deal with the entire person and not just their thoughts. While no therapy is going to exclude the importance of behavior, CBT balances the importance of dealing with cognitive distortions and behavior and allowing the two to work together to complement and support positive feelings and emotions.

This makes CBT not only an effective therapy but one that can continue to grow with the person as they begin to appreciate better thoughts, better moods, better feelings and of course, better behavior.

Where behavior modification falls short, dealing effectively with moods and feelings on a cognitive level can then interact successfully with improved behavior.

This allows the therapist to not only function to address maladaptive behavior but to identify the causal links between cognitive distortions, acting out, and the appearance of negative and/or maladaptive behavior.

Therapists are also free to teach patients the importance of dealing with all aspects of their humanity. Extending mental health therapy to people is a process that not only involves cognition but the ability to recognize what cognitive distortions are causing pain in their lives.

For a person that has grown accustomed to cognitive distortions, it can take some time and even hard work to eventually get to the point where their behavior begins to change effectively.

This has a very positive impact, especially over time when dealing with people that are suffering from various degrees of mental illness.

Some of the more difficult and painful behaviors and thoughts can be challenged not immediately, but on a graduated scale that can be dealt with effectively by the patient. Therefore, CBT and its main goals are easily met, unlike some therapies that require useless repetition without much positive gain.

Effective Considerations for The Assessment

Once the assessment has been made, baselines have been taken, behavior modification suggested, as well as cognitive therapy introduced, we are now free to look at the larger picture because CBT involves many other aspects in a patient's life.

Treatment is best *not done in a vacuum* and should always involve important people to the patient. Even if the patient does not need to make all of the social criteria below part of his or her treatment, all of these aspects should be taken into consideration by the therapist and those that work on the treatment care plan:

- *Family & friends*—in order to preserve the integrity and privacy of the patient, the only family and friends involved should be the ones that are aware of the care plan. Here we also can involve people with just enough information to allow them to contribute their provided function. For example, a family member may only need to know that they wish to participate in a daily exercise to improve the person's mood and health, not that this item is actually ordered on a care plan.

- *Job/ workplace*—the only interaction that members at work should have with any patient should be in the form of stress reduction and should be done so carefully and cautiously through superiors. Changing job responsibilities slightly or moving the person to a new division with less overall responsibility or a completely new way of doing work that would relieve prior anxieties of the patient could involve other peers. Despite most people's fears, this type of adjunct therapy is done frequently and quietly at most workplaces that offer the least restrictive environment for their workers.

- *Societal position*—the patient may have responsibilities in society, such as sitting on a board, involvement with the local Chamber of Commerce, etc. Patients can temporarily step down or have another family member take up responsibilities or reduce the amount of time devoted to such societal positions.

- *Personality*—the strength of personality is also important because this dictates exactly how the patient will interact with other people.
- Personality distortions—once they are corrected, can alter the way the person perceives reality and the way other people perceive this new aspect of an older or emerging personality.

- *Personal beliefs*—religious and/or ethical beliefs almost always impact behavior and therefore, should be a source of strength and not something restrictive in nature unless the person is emerging from an oppressive cultlike religion that is at the center of their disorders. Again, this is a thought process for the therapist and the patient.

- *Professional beliefs*—some patients hold very strong professional beliefs that can impact their behavior. For example, OCD people are often compelled to behave in repetitive manners that, once cured, may seem to reduce their overall effectiveness and could impact their job performance.

- *Other considerations*—numerous other considerations can impact diagnostics and/or suggested therapies that should be part of an overall baseline and screening. The key is to establish a diagnostic snapshot that best allows the therapist to choose a course of action along with the patient who will also understand the importance is of managing the overall impact on their lives.

The key to understanding all of this is to realize that as therapy progresses people begin to change. The idea is to make the changes positive once possible and limit any negative impact on the person's overall life scheme.

Occasionally the importance of mental health far outweighs a person's current job, and after therapy, they may need to seek a different type or style of living contingent on the requirements for their new perspectives on health.

Intervention & Treatment Analysis

Both cognitive and behavioral therapy require an understanding as to the correct type of intervention and analysis for treatment based on events in someone's life.

Intervention and treatment analysis require that we understand the steps and considerations first and then determine the best approaches to this process.

Multiple treatments can and should be proposed based on:

- The best type of cognitive therapy.

- The best type of behavioral therapy.
- The best type of management of both the emotions and feelings during the other two therapies.

It is not the express goal of CBT to manage all aspects, all the time. Remember our main focus is on determining the best type of intervention first after we take our baseline.

For example, Randy has constant panic attacks while he is in public and finds it difficult to talk to other people. The panic attacks happen anytime he is surrounded by people he does not know, and has to give an account of who he is or what he needs.

What most people would consider average everyday behavior, like going to the bank and withdrawing money, is an extremely awkward and difficult situation for Randy.

The therapist has proposed a form of systematic desensitization to teach him ways to learn how to deal with scenarios and situations of escalating stress.

This is a form of intervention and treatment analysis that the therapist has made. Such decisions should never be made in a vacuum, and require a firm baseline and understanding that this should be and is the best possible overall treatment.

Lacking sufficient background information, the beginning and/or intervention series requires several understandings:

- What information has been accrued during the baseline study that suggests the therapy or therapies that you wish to use are the best?

- What type of psychosocial focus should your therapy have, if any?

- Should the therapy or therapies that you choose to involve scenarios that are painful yet necessary to help the potential patient through their disorders?

- What social tools can you use during an intervention and should the intervention be coupled with immediate therapy constructs? Why?

- What will be the impact of the therapy on the person's thinking, behavior, and feelings?

- Is it necessary to invoke discomfort during any of this process and how could this be avoided, if necessary? Should it be avoided at first?

- What are some of the top pieces of literature in the area and/or white papers suggesting based on your current situation as a therapist with the current patient that you have?

- Do you require the use of other professionals such as a drug addiction specialist, to reach a certain level of functioning to administer therapy?

All of these scenarios involve an understanding of exactly what you're going to do before you begin the use of any therapy and if the intervention becomes confrontational or more passive in nature contingent on disorders.

The good news is that simply changing cognition can always be the first starting step before you begin to affect or impact behavior. Of course, this is contingent on a scenario in which behavior is not currently destructive and thus needs to be ceased immediately, such as hard-core alcoholism, drug abuse, etc. Ultimately the term "intervention" needs not to be draconian in nature. Passive intervention can work just as well.

The Power of CBT to Destroy Negative Feelings

Therapists can now tap various behavioral models via the baseline information and use them to spot and reduce critical behaviors that are disturbing the client and causing breakdowns in thought reactive models.

In other words, now is the time for interventions based on assessment and to utilize top strategies with tools like thought stopping, passive confrontation, and, cognitive modeling.

Understand that the main function of CBT is the removal of erroneous thinking. One of the best ways to attack this is to look for the most common cognitive distortions.

Erroneous thinking is the result of cognitive distortions plus possible misunderstandings based on feelings and emotions. The impact on the behavioral aspect is the result of the cognitive distortions manifested into erroneous thinking that can also be linked with problematic feelings and emotions. Let us delve into this area of cognitive distortions and explain in detail the necessity for correcting erroneous thinking.

Chapter 7 Mountain Meditation

This meditation is one of my favorites, and I find that a lot of people feel in tune with it. During this practice, we are going to imagine being arock-solid mountain, surrounded by nature and habited by animals, plants, and trees.

Once the image is well painted inside our mind, we will add the element of time, allowing it to pass in a constant and smooth way. We are going to feel the different seasons, starting from the Summer, and we are going to experience differentemotions. It is important to notice how the mountain remains still and solid, even during the most difficult times, offering a safe place for animals and plants.

By becoming self-aware of our mountain-ness, we can face daily difficulties with new energy and a rejuvenated spirit. Doing this practice once a week for a month is ideal to see the most benefits. Also, as you will see, it is a pretty interesting and fun experience!

Let's get started!

Find a comfortable, relaxed, and balanced position. Permit yourself to be completely present for yourself, and let your body and mind calm down until they become soft and relaxed.

Breathe in, feel relaxed...
breathe out, feel calm.

Breathe in, feel relaxed...
breathe out, feel calm.

Breathe in, feel relaxed...
breathe out, feel calm.

Breathe in, feel relaxed...
breathe out, feel calm.

Allow the mind to distance itself from all thoughts and orientate awareness on your breath. Breathe naturally and do not force a specific rhythm. Let your breath come and go.

Carefully, now, drive your attention from the breath to the space in which you are.

Feel the energy and atmosphere of this space as it permeates all of your beings. Notice the noises in the background. Maybe there is a clock ticking; maybe cars are passing just outside your windows. Whatever you feel, it is fine. Let your attention rest on the external.

Breathe in, feel relaxed...
breathe out, feel calm.

Breathe in, feel relaxed...
breathe out, feel calm.

Breathe in, feel relaxed...
breathe out, feel calm.

Breathe in, feel relaxed...
breathe out, feel calm.
Now bring the attention back to the breath. Take your time and you will naturally reach a place of warmth and ease.

There is nothing to do here, nothing to think or to worry about. Just rest your attention on the breath, following each inhalation and exhalation with curiosity, falling into the rhythm of your very own body.

If you want, you can place your hands on your belly. This will help you enter in connection with the natural movement of the air entering through your nose and exciting trough the mouth.

Breathe in, feel relaxed...
breathe out, feel calm.

Breathe in, feel relaxed...
breathe out, feel calm.

Breathe in, feel relaxed...
breathe out, feel calm.

Breathe in, feel relaxed...
breathe out, feel calm.

Breathe in, feel relaxed...
breathe out, feel calm.
Breathe in, feel relaxed...
breathe out, feel calm.

Breathe in, feel relaxed...
breathe out, feel calm.

Breathe in, feel relaxed...
breathe out, feel calm.
I will give you a few more minutes to get into this zone, as we will then begin the actual practice.

Breathe in, feel relaxed...
breathe out, feel calm.

Breathe in, feel relaxed...
breathe out, feel calm.

Breathe in, feel relaxed...
breathe out, feel calm.

Breathe in, feel relaxed...
breathe out, feel calm.

Breathe in, feel relaxed...
breathe out, feel calm.

Breathe in, feel relaxed...
breathe out, feel calm.

Breathe in, feel relaxed...
breathe out, feel calm.

Breathe in, feel relaxed...
breathe out, feel calm.

Breathe in, feel relaxed...
breathe out, feel calm.

Breathe in, feel relaxed...
breathe out, feel calm.

Breathe in, feel relaxed...
breathe out, feel calm.

Breathe in, feel relaxed…
breathe out, feel calm.

Breathe in, feel relaxed…
breathe out, feel calm.

Breathe in, feel relaxed…

breathe out, feel calm.

Breathe in, feel relaxed…
breathe out, feel calm.

Breathe in, feel relaxed…
breathe out, feel calm.

Now start imagining a mountain, a big and rock-solid mountain. If you have a favorite one, you can picture it as well. Maybe it is a place where you go on a regular basis or maybe it is a mountain you have only seen on video. Just take a few minutes to paint it as clearly as you can in your mind. Try to grasp every detail, from the height to the temperature. The more you can add, the greater the benefits.

Breathe in, feel relaxed…
breathe out, feel calm.

Breathe in, feel relaxed…
breathe out, feel calm.

Breathe in, feel relaxed…

breathe out, feel calm.

Breathe in, feel relaxed…

breathe out, feel calm.

Breathe in, feel relaxed…

breathe out, feel calm.

Breathe in, feel relaxed…

breathe out, feel calm.

Breathe in, feel relaxed…

breathe out, feel calm.

Breathe in, feel relaxed…

breathe out, feel calm.

Once you have the image in your mind, we can get started. It is Summer, and all the animals are coming towards you finding peace under the shadow you provide them. Tourists and hikers take pictures of you and their kids run up and down your trails. Trees and flowers are nourished by your soil and paint you in a dark green color.

Everything is perfect, nice, and cozy, and it seems that this beautiful feeling will never end.

Breathe in, feel relaxed…
breathe out, feel calm.

Breathe in, feel relaxed...
breathe out, feel calm.

Breathe in, feel relaxed...
breathe out, feel calm.

Breathe in, feel relaxed...
breathe out, feel calm.

Breathe in, feel relaxed...
breathe out, feel calm.

Breathe in, feel relaxed...
breathe out, feel calm.

Breathe in, feel relaxed...
breathe out, feel calm.

Breathe in, feel relaxed...

breathe out, feel calm.

Breathe in, feel relaxed...
breathe out, feel calm.

Breathe in, feel relaxed...
breathe out, feel calm.

Breathe in, feel relaxed...
breathe out, feel calm.

Breathe in, feel relaxed...
breathe out, feel calm.

Breathe in, feel relaxed...
breathe out, feel calm.

Breathe in, feel relaxed...
breathe out, feel calm.

Breathe in, feel relaxed...
breathe out, feel calm.

Breathe in, feel relaxed...
breathe out, feel calm.

Time goes by very quickly, and sooner than later, fewer and fewer people come and take pictures of you. The beautiful trees are now losing their leaves, and the animals are seeking repair in the valley, leaving you almost alone. The last flowers are perishing and your soil is not a good source of nourishment anymore. You think that this feeling will never end.

Breathe in, feel relaxed...
breathe out, feel calm.

Breathe in, feel relaxed...
breathe out, feel calm.

Breathe in, feel relaxed...
breathe out, feel calm.

Breathe in, feel relaxed...
breathe out, feel calm.

Breathe in, feel relaxed...
breathe out, feel calm.

Breathe in, feel relaxed...

breathe out, feel calm.

Breathe in, feel relaxed...
breathe out, feel calm.

Breathe in, feel relaxed...
breathe out, feel calm.

Now Winter comes. The snow starts coming down, covering all your trails and rocks. No flowers are popping up and the trees are now entirely brown. Their leaves are on the ground, covered by snow. The temperature is freezing and all the animals are now far away, trying to survive this season as best as they can. People stay far away from you because they are scared of avalanches. They look at you with a deep sense of respect but are not willing to visit you for the time being. You think that this feeling will never end.

Breathe in, feel relaxed...
breathe out, feel calm.

Breathe in, feel relaxed...
breathe out, feel calm.

Breathe in, feel relaxed...
breathe out, feel calm.

Breathe in, feel relaxed...
breathe out, feel calm.

Breathe in, feel relaxed...
breathe out, feel calm.

Breathe in, feel relaxed...
breathe out, feel calm.

Breathe in, feel relaxed...
breathe out, feel calm.

Breathe in, feel relaxed...
breathe out, feel calm.

Slowly things start to change, and you are noticing it with new hope. The snow is melting, the trees becoming green again and beautiful wildflowers are popping up all over you. Soon enough, the first hikers are taking pictures of you again and everyone is telling how gorgeous you are. The sun is getting brighter, the days are getting longer. The animals are coming back and are dancing for you on your beautiful trails. It is Spring at its finest, and you think that this feeling will never end.

Breathe in, feel relaxed...
breathe out, feel calm.

Breathe in, feel relaxed...
breathe out, feel calm.

Breathe in, feel relaxed...
breathe out, feel calm.

Breathe in, feel relaxed...
breathe out, feel calm.

Breathe in, feel relaxed...
breathe out, feel calm.

Breathe in, feel relaxed...
breathe out, feel calm.

Breathe in, feel relaxed...
breathe out, feel calm.

Breathe in, feel relaxed...
breathe out, feel calm.

And in a blink of an eye, everything starts all over again. Summer, Fall, Winter, Spring, and then Summer again, in a never-ending cycle. And no matter what happens around you, you are still there, feeling strong and solid as a mountain.

I would like you to bring this feeling with you for the rest of the week, as you are truly capable of amazing things when you tap into the unlimited source of energy that is your soul.

Breathe in, feel relaxed...
breathe out, feel calm.

Breathe in, feel relaxed...
breathe out, feel calm.

Breathe in, feel relaxed...
breathe out, feel calm.

Breathe in, feel relaxed...
breathe out, feel calm.

Breathe in, feel relaxed...
breathe out, feel calm.

Breathe in, feel relaxed...
breathe out, feel calm.

Breathe in, feel relaxed...
breathe out, feel calm.

Breathe in, feel relaxed...
breathe out, feel calm.
Now bring the attention back to the body and start feeling your arms and legs once again. You can close your hands or move your fingers just to take control of the space around you.

Please, keep the eyes closed for now and enjoy the beautiful moment you are living. You have given yourself the time to feel better and that is absolutely incredible.

Breathe in, feel relaxed...
breathe out, feel calm.
Breathe in, feel relaxed...
breathe out, feel calm.

Breathe in, feel relaxed...
breathe out, feel calm.

Breathe in, feel relaxed...
breathe out, feel calm.

Now become aware of the environment around you once again. Feel the different sounds, the temperature of the room you are in and once you are ready, open the eyes again.

Chapter 8 Meditation to Achieve Your Life Goals

Single-focus meditation involves meditating with your eyes wide open. In the previous two meditation techniques, I described practices where you have to close your eyes. With single-focus meditation, you remain completely aware of the visuals around you while your eyes are wide open. You then look at what's around you, and you focus on one particular detail of the scene.

For example, I'm writing this book from a café and I'm looking out at the river right beside the café. I notice that there's a bridge and underneath the bridge, there's some water. Using this technique, I would zero in on one particular detail. Maybe I'd just look at the lower part of the bridge or maybe I'd just look at one aspect of the river. Whatever the case may be, I would reduce my field of vision and zero in on one particular detail.

The goal here is to simply empty your mind by focusing all your attention on one small detail. When you do this, you actually unclench your mind. Typically, people are juggling many different facts, details, and issues with their minds.

As I've mentioned previously, the mind is like a muscle. The more things you worry about, the more tension you put on your mental muscle. Eventually, if you reach a point where you're thinking of so many things, the muscle actually just clamps up and just can't let go. It just gets clogged and you feel really stuck. You're still thinking and your mind still works, but it has slowed down and it's really unable to let you move on.

This effect is very similar to a runner's cramp. When you're running, there's some tension in your leg muscles, but due to a variety of reasons, if your muscles can't cope up with the different stresses you put on your muscles, they cramp up. Each step forward is uncomfortable, if not flat out painful!

Single-focus meditation is a very powerful meditation practice that enables you to unclench your mind. By simply flushing out all the other information that is normally in your mind's pipeline and focusing on one element, you can't help but feel relaxed.

Focus Without Judging

Another key element to this practice is that you only need to focus on the detail without judging it. Again, back to my example, I'm looking at the lower part of the bridge in front of me and I just allow myself to look at all the different details. I look at the colors, I look at how the sunlight is bouncing off the bridge's bricks, and I leave it at that.

There's no need for analysis. I don't have to compare the bricks with bricks I've seen before. I don't have to make any conclusions regarding the workmanship involved in building the bridge. I don't have to concern myself with the issue of whether the city got ripped off by contractors due to the quality and placement of the bricks. I simply don't allow myself to get worried about or caught up in any issue involving the bridge's bricks.

Similarly, there's no need to connect that image with some sort of deep philosophical or emotional meaning. I don't have to place meaning in the faded look of the bricks. I don't have to view the bricks as an analogy to my career, the choices I've made, my relationships, or anything else in my life.

I simply allow myself to just appreciate a particular detail for itself.

You stay at this level of focus for the length of your meditation. When you do this, you prevent yourself from judging your thoughts. Why? Mental images don't form.

You're basically just stuck looking at particular details and the normal process where your mind thinks of different issues and where different mental images coming to the fore doesn't happen. Best of all, you're not putting an emotional layer on these mental images since this process is not taking place. You're not judging, you're not getting caught up in any kind of emotional connection, and you're not doing much of anything at all although your brain is highly-focused.

The best part of single-focus meditation is that you're in full control. It's like being in charge of a laser, and you can point it to whichever direction you want.

Basic Operations

With this technique, you don't need a special room. You don't need to separate yourself from other people. You can be in a crowded café like where I am right now and practice single-focus meditation. People probably wouldn't even notice that you're doing it. They might just think that you're daydreaming or are deep in thought.

It's All About Focus

The secret to this technique, however, is extended focus. You have to make sure that you focused on that particular detail and not let whatever is happening around you interrupt your attention. If you're able to do this, your mind will relax while at the same time boosting your overall level of mental focus. Your ability to pick up on 'micro-details' increases tremendously. You can become a more astute observer when not meditating.

Chapter 9 Guided Meditation to End Anxiety Attacks

Another major reason why most people find it difficult to sleep or to obtain deep sleep is due to the mental panic attacks that they suffer from as they attempt to relax their minds. This is even more common amongst individuals who have some form of anxiety disorder and are prone to worry, negative thinking or nervousness. In fact, because such disorders tend to center around negative thoughts such as insecurities, disabilities, and handicaps, they can effectively be dealt with when confronted with positive thinking exercises like meditation and mindfulness exercises.

For today's exercise, we will be focusing on a relaxation technique that allows your mind to delve into the root causes of anxiety, how they pertain to you as an individual, and how to prevent the buildup of such thoughts in the future. By filtering our thought process, guided mindful meditation can help bring an end to anxiety and call forth a sense of inner peace.

Meditative Guide to End Anxiety Attacks

As before, find yourself a quiet corner in which you can seat yourself for about 30 minutes without being disturbed. Remember that the process iskey to a good meditation, so try to ensure that you are somewhere where you are both comfortable and isolated so that the guide has the opportunity to run through before you are called away.

You are now ready to start your meditative guide. As you begin, draw a long breath into your body until you have filled your lungs to the fullest, and after holding the breath for five whole seconds, expel it powerfully through your mouth to purge yourself of negativity.

Repeat the process two more times.

As you do this, remind yourself of what you are doing today and what your purpose is—your intention today is to dissolve and disperse the anxiety that arises within you, and in order to do that, we will be targeting negative waste within you and building up positive energy.

Breathe.
Hold.
Release.

You are able to open yourself to a new empowered way of being if you so choose.
As you draw your breath in, you can feel your body and mind start to slow down and relax. You are letting go of stress and its binders so that your body is capable of being a clear conduit through which you can channel positivity and flush out negative holds on your subconscious.

Breathe.
Hold.
Release.

Start by identifying and releasing your panic. Breathe in sharply and, as you do, feel yourself relaxing into that specific puff of air as it travels through your body.
Hold. You are in control, so remind yourself that this is now your world and ergo your reality within which you have the ability to easily and effortlessly free yourself from all negative realms.

Release your breath. As you do, unhook yourself from the panic that has held onto you.

Breathe.
Hold.
Release.

Remind yourself that you are now in control, and you are powerful and present. You are not swayed and cannot be wavered.

Breathe.
Hold.
Release.

Your life is now peaceful and calm.

Breathe.
Hold.
Release.

You are safe.
You are in control.

You are free from the need for panic. Panic has no hold on you. Panic is not a part of you.

Breathe.
Hold.
Release.

Imagine that you are floating down a river.in a small wooden boat—simply floating aimlessly wherever the current may go.

As you live back on your boat, you find before you a warm, comforting the sky with soft white clouds, cushioning the sun, reminding you of the carefree summer days that you enjoyed as a child.

Breathe.
Hold.
Release.

You are safe.
You are in control.

Remember that with each breath, you release your worries are also floating away into nothingness.

There is nothing that binds you.
No pressures.
No time constraints.
No worries.
Nothing.
Breathe.
Now, repeat after me: I am loved and enough. There are no fears that overwhelm me and no panic that can overtake me.

I am calm and centered, and with my every breath, my mind clears and I am at peace.

Repeat it again in your heart: I am loved and enough. There are no fears that overwhelm me and no panic that can overtake me.

I am calm and centered, and with my every breath, my mind clears and I am at peace.

Breathe.
Hold.
Release.

The storm in your mind has calmed, and as you open your eyes, you will feel like a happier, more whole version of yourself.

Chapter 10 Guided Meditation for Super Motivation

Another major area that is affected by the lack of proper sleep is productivity. When it comes to productivity, in addition to a lack of sleep, anxiety also creates a buildup of negative vibrations which, in turn, destroy your natural motivational force. As a result, when we are faced with any major task or even when we are faced with the combination of small tasks, you will find that there is a noticeable lack of positive energy generated in regard to that specific task. This lack of motivation is why meditative intervention is so important.

Think of all the times that what seems like a simple task to you is actually all-consuming to others. Not only have you been lazy and lethargic, but you have also failed to acknowledge that this is an important matter that needs to get done. Instead, your mind goes into a defensive mode where you begin to list the other things that you need to get done in an attempt to justify why you were not doing this particular task. Clearly, this is not how the rest of your life can be allowed to go by. What youneed at this moment is a strong dose of motivation to help you help yourself.

Which is exactly what we are going to be working on!

Meditative Guide for Super Motivation

As you prepare yourself to step forward into your guided meditation, it is important that, as always, you start by finding yourself a meditation-friendly environment. Take a deep breath and look around yourself to find a corner where you will not be disturbed for the next ten to fifteen minutes.

For motivation exercises, it is important to seat yourself in a well-lit area, which is why a wide-open window or a clean terrace is optimum. If, however, you do not have access to either of these places, just set the alarm for fifteen minutes early and take a pit stop at a neighborhood park on your way to work. The open spaces and the proper wind channels will help you breathe more clearly and will also help you focus your mind without feeling trapped or suffocated.

You are now ready to start your meditative guide. Start by drawing a deep breath in through your nose and releasing swiftly through the bridge of your mouth.

Breathe in sharply,

and exhale.

Repeat this exercise three additional times.

Breathe in sharply,

and exhale.

Breathe in sharply,

and exhale.

Breathe in sharply,

and exhale.

Breathe.

Relax.

The constant noise surrounding you is beginning to fade away.

And as it does, you will start to realize that you have dozens of tasks that you need to accomplish, and yet, at the same time, you feel unmotivated to attend to a single one.

Breathe in.

Hold.

And exhale.

Breathe in deeply, and relax your shoulders and neck.

As you feel your mind and body slowly unwinding, focus your mind on the knots of tension in your shoulders and mentally relax.

Envision your tasks for the day.

Make a list in your mind's eye, and as you go through it, ask yourself, what you have let hold you back.

Breathe in.

Hold.

And exhale.

Your body is now slowly starting to feel heavy as you feel more and more relaxed.

Breathe in.

Hold.

And exhale.

You are a strong, motivated person.

You enjoy all the challenges, and challenges do not scare or intimidate you, because you are motivated to succeed.

The only option you have before you is a success, and your motivation comes from within you.

You are a motivated person.

You are a happy and motivated person who enjoys everything that they do.

Your goal is what motivates you, and you work continuously until your motivation matches your goal.

You are strong and motivated.

Negativity is repelled by you because you are strong and motivated.

You are a motivated person.

You are motivated to achieve and to do all that needs to be done.

You are motivated to succeed.

You are always motivated, and motivation is a state of being for you.

Now, repeat after me: I am strong and motivated. My motivation will push me to complete every task that I am set. There are no negative forces that can hold me back from being motivated and fulfilling all my tasks.

Motivation comes to me easily, and I am always motivated to motivate myself and others.

Repeat it again, in your heart: I am strong and motivated. My motivation will push me to complete every task that I am set. There are no

negative forces that can hold me back from being motivated and fulfilling all my tasks.
Motivation comes to me easily, and I am always motivated to motivate myself and others.

Breathe.
Hold.
Release.

Slowly open your eyes.
You are now alert and motivated by the tasks that you have set for yourself and seek to complete them in the most efficient manner possible.

Chapter 11 Guided Meditation to Help With Stress Relief

With concerns regarding mental health arising, you will soon find that the major players, such as fear, despair, and negativity, all tend to stem from the same root factor—stress. Meditation has a wonderful ability to help with stress management. Not only does guided meditation allows you to help build your mental resilience, but it is also an extremely effective tool to help relax your body and mind on a more immediate basis.

Stress relief meditation, in particular, can be used not only to help improve your mental state of being but also to help you release the physical tension you feel in your own body due to anxiety.

Meditative Guide to Help With Stress Relief

In this particular form of meditation, we will be dealing with finding a way to release your inner struggles, worries, sorrows, and stress. To begin, you want to create a peaceful atmosphere around you.

Surround yourself with dim lights, set your room to a comfortable temperature, and, if you choose, light a candle or set out essential oils to help bring forth a calming aura.

You are now ready to start your meditative guide. Before you close your eyes, look closely around you, and make a careful mental note of the things you see. Once you are done, close your eyes and focus on a fixed point in your mind's eye. Then, purge yourself of negativity and negative thoughts by carefully breathing into the count of five, holding your breath until the count of four, and then releasing to the count of three.

Breathe in.
Hold.
Release.

Breathe in.
Hold.
Release.

Breathe in.
Hold.
Release.

With your eyes closed, focus your mind on the sounds that you hear around you. Look past these sounds, and beyond them, you will find the voices of the people you love most dearly. Your loved ones and your well-wishers are all gathered here around you in a circle, amidst which you are seated.
The sounds you hear around you are slowly morphing into the voices of the people you love.

Breathe in.
Hold.
Release.

Focus on the voices—the voices are talking to you.

As you do so, start to identify the fears that are holding you in place. What scares you? What intimidates you? What do you fear?
Mentally assign a bold color to each of these fears and color them in so that you can see how strong

their hold on you is.

Breathe in.
Hold.
Release.

See the colors swarm you and intertwine with the other—fear into insecurity, insecurity into greed, greed into falsehoods, and so on and so forth. As you do start to focus on the voice once again, try to hear what they are saying.

Breathe in.
Hold.
Release.

Notice that they are reminding you of your worth.

You are good.

You are kind.

You are loved.

You are needed.

You are cherished.

You are wanted.

Breathe in.
Hold.
Release.

Every voice is manifesting in the form of a bright white light that is blasting through the bold reds, blues, and greens of your fears and is opening tiny breaks through which you can release yourself.

Breathe in.
Hold.
Release.

Remind yourself that the love and belief that they have in you is enough to set you free.
As you do this, travel through your body with your next breath and do so physically for yourself.

Breathe in.

As you feel the breath travel down through your shoulders, consciously let the tension loose, feel your shoulders flex backward, and release the weight on your shoulders as you allow the energy to flow through your entire being.

Each particle of energy is now changing from a chain to a bright searing white light which is radiating through your body.

Breathe in.
Hold.
Release.

Remind yourself of the things that are shifting inside of you as you feel the transformation takes place.

You are calm and relaxed.

You are loved and respected.

You are letting go of all of the unwanted fears that hold you back and instead, you are filling yourself with stillness.

Breathe in.
Hold.
Release.

Remember that with each breath, you are releasing your concerns, and with each release, you are becoming lighter and lighter until you are but the weight of a feather adrift in the wind.

Repeat after me: I am supported and loved, and stressful situations do not scare me - they merely challenge me.

I am calm and centered, and calmness washes over me with every breath that I take.

Repeat it again, in your heart: I am supported and loved, and stressful situations do not scare me— they merely challenge me.

I am calm and centered, and calmness washes over me with every breath that I take.

Breathe in.
Hold.
Release.

As you slowly open your eyes, you will feel a physical burn shift from your shoulders and, instead of stress and pain, you will feel only thankfulness and courage.

Chapter 12 Meditation to Calm the Mind

Meditation is a common exercise people use to quiet their minds and reduce stress. It has worked wonders for so many people, possibly because there are so many different types and techniques, making it easy for someone to find a kind of meditation that works for them. From mindfulness practices to yoga and positive self-talk, meditation can form to a person's individual needs and help them find calm and peace-of-mind they might be missing while dealing with their symptoms. It can be difficult to get into at first, but once a person masters meditating, they often see marked improvements in their mood and stress levels.

Yoga is a common exercise that people might not always associate with meditating, but ancient religions created it as a way to do just that. The different yoga practices all focus on making the mind aware of the body as it stretches and strengthens the muscles. It focuses on deep breathing to relax a person so they can achieve a deeper stretch and have a more peaceful experience. Many yoga classes even directly incorporate meditation into the poses by instructing people to listen to their breathing and focus on how it affects their bodies.

Meditating can be a simple way to reduce stress, quiet the mind, and become more focused during the day. It can reduce physical pain by working to lower stress hormones and responses in the body to feel both mentally and physically healthier. This chapter explores common meditation practices, how yoga can reduce stress, all the ways meditation can help someone reduce anxiety, and directions on how to use meditation effectively in your life.

Common Practices

Meditation can be a great way to reduce stress and limit the effects of anxiety. It is also useful because it can be practiced at any time and in any place, making it a great tool for people who experience symptoms in public. Teaching your mind to calm down and focus can not only reduce anxiety but also stress and worry as well. Meditation is usually considered complementary to therapy because it can help a person get into the right mindset to begin examining themselves and their symptoms. It can also help them remain calm during difficult exercises such as confronting fears or identifying triggers.

The point of meditation is to focus the mind on something simple instead of letting negative thoughts turn into messy, knotted bunches in your brain. Meditation takes people through exercises where they can start to pull at the strings of these knots and slowly untangle them until they feel at peace again. There are many different meditation practices you can use, including some physical activities and some resting mental activities, that can help you calm down and focus. Some people prefer to do activities where they sit still and focus, and others like the distraction of moving during their meditation.

Guided meditation is one type of sedentary meditation that can be especially helpful for beginners. In this type, a person's voice moves you through meditation by telling you what to focus on and what to do with your body. It can help people with no meditation experience to learn the basics and find a natural rhythm that they can later keep on their own. Mantra meditation is similar to this tactic, but it does not involve another person. The meditator finds a word or phrase that helps them to calm down and then repeats it during their meditation and lets the words become their focus.

Mindfulness meditation is a way to employ two calming techniques at once and engage all of your senses. It focuses on increasing awareness of your surroundings and your body as a means of accepting the world you live in for what it is. This type of meditation can also help people to practice living in the moment instead of worrying about the past or future. People typically focus on their body, such as the rhythm of their breathing and the deepness of their breath, how their muscles feel when they take in air, and release it. When an anxious thought pops into your head during meditation, this type suggests you acknowledge its existence and then let it go; don't waste time or energy entertaining all its possibilities.

More physical versions of meditation include Tai Chi and yoga. Tai Chi focuses on slow, deliberate movements while taking purposeful breaths. It can help people learn how to breathe during a physical response to anxiety, teach calmness, and improve balance. Yoga can be a little more intense than Tai Chi, depending on what type of practice a person is attempting. It focuses on listening to the body and responding to its needs through a series of poses intended to stretch and release different muscles. Yoga often ends with a few minutes to lie in silence and feel the muscles of your body and your breathing work together to support you.

How it helps

Yoga combines the three main relaxation techniques that people with anxiety and panic disorders frequently utilize: deep breathing, muscle relaxation, and visualization. These three things create a stress-free, peace-inducing atmosphere that makes it easy to let go of stress and worry. Yoga has been known to help people reduce stress, lower blood pressure, and lower heart rate by pairing exercise with meditation. Its anxious roots have always focused on finding inner peace and becoming one with the earth, helping some people feel more connected to their environment instead of afraid of it.

Because yoga is a physical activity, it can help promote mindfulness and relieve some of the physical symptoms of anxiety. Often, anxious people suffer from stiff or sore muscles from holding tension in their body for prolonged periods. Yoga can help them stretch those muscles and relieve some of the tension they feel daily.

The goal of yoga is to stretch, lengthen, and strengthen muscles as a form of meditation. The physical response to different poses gives a person something to focus on instead of the thoughts running through their head. It can help some people feel more in touch with their bodies and become more aware of their signals. It is a good outlet for someone who wants a more intense meditative work out than Tai Chi or walking because they can definitely work up a sweat doing yoga. Finding the right type for their skill level and based on desired results can also be helpful to find one that gives them just enough exercise to feel like they've accomplished something.

Joining a yoga class can also be a great way to meet new people and interact with someone every day.

This can be great for people who are trying not to withdraw from others and push their social boundaries each week. During the class, they can quiet their mind enough to build up the courage to speak to someone after the lesson is over.

There are many different types of yoga that could be beneficial for a beginner, such as Hatha or Asana yoga. Hatha yoga has a slower pace than most practices and easier movements. It is often focused a little more on meditating and being aware of the body than deeply stretching muscles. Asana yoga is a bit more fast-paced and focuses on movement and stretching a little more than meditation, but usually ends with time to meditate and reflect on the openness of your muscles after practice.

Beginners can sometimes be intimidated if they walk into a yoga class and do not know what to expect. All types of yoga are made up of a sequence of poses that are combined to move your body through a logical pattern of stretching. They all come together to help release tension and relax the muscles while also promoting flexibility and strength. Poses can range from lying on the floor to standing on one leg with arms outstretched. Yoga can help people with a variety of chronic conditions such as anxiety, panic disorder, or illnesses that cause significant pain.

Meditation can help both mental and physical health by giving people a sense of balance, calm, and inner peace. These things can carry throughout their day beyond their meditation session to help them feel calm and in control. Sometimes this feeling alone is enough to help someone cope with their anxiety. It can also help people to clear their minds of the clutter and stress they carry with them during the day. Having a blank slate to start the day with can make the onslaught of tasks feel much more manageable and keep a person from feeling like they are overwhelmed or out of control.

Taking time to meditate can also help someone see a new perspective about something they were maybe obsessing over or worrying about. Sometimes being able to see a problem in a new light can help you feel less anxious about it and understand it better. If a person can take the time during the day to look for new ways to view their anxiety, it can make it easier to deal with when it flares up.

Meditation even promotes an increased self-awareness, which can help some people focus on the present during the day. Being able to keep the mind in the present moment and not wander into regrets of the past or the possibilities of the future, can be an incredibly effective way for people to avoid anxiety panic attacks. Along with this awareness can come patience, tolerance, imagination, and creativity. All of these qualities can encourage a person to be kinder to themselves and others and possibly even be more productive at work because their brains are free to explore, unencumbered by negative thoughts.

Mental peace can sometimes even aid in physical recovery, especially those illnesses that are worsened by stress. By calming people, meditation can help to reduce inflammation in the body that is caused by stress hormones. Reducing this internal inflammation can often relieve a considerable amount of pain for people. Aside from pain, research suggests meditating can help people who suffer from a wide range of symptoms, including asthma, heart disease, high blood pressure, sleep problems, and headaches. It could be because all of these symptoms can be worsened by stress and once that is alleviated the symptoms are alleviated too.

In addition to mental and physical health, meditating can even help someone lengthen their attention span. This can be extremely helpful both at work and in school, especially if a person suffers from an attention disorder or has trouble focusing their mind on the conversation and not on their own anxiety. It can also help older adults who are starting to suffer from memory loss due to their age. This is because when a person improves their attention span and their clarity of mind, it can help the brain retain characteristics of a younger person such as holding on to and being able to recall memories.

Finally, perhaps the best benefit of meditating is that people don't have to do it at home. If you are anxious before a big meeting, take a moment at your desk to meditate and focus on your breathing until you feel you have calmed down enough to step into the boardroom. You don't have to wait for an appointment or have someone guide you, meditation is always available when you need it.

Meditation can be difficult to get used to, especially if your brain is used to traveling a mile a minute.

Racing thoughts can be difficult to quiet without a little practice, so people should remember that their first couple of attempts to meditate might not go as seamlessly as they hoped for.

The key to effective meditation can be to find a time in your day where it fits rather seamlessly. This can help you avoid stressing about when you will ever find time to meditate, which is the opposite of the exercise's goal. If you are a morning person, you might want to wake up a few minutes early to sit in peace for a moment before starting your daily routine. If you know you always have extra time on your lunch break, that might be a good time to sneak in five minutes of meditation. Even if you are only doing it in the moments before you fallasleep at night, finding any time to quiet your mind during the day can be beneficial to managing anxiety.

Some people might feel confused about how long they are supposed to meditate. This factor depends entirely on them and how much time they have during the day to dedicate to meditation, how long they would like to meditate for, and what are their attitudes toward the exercise. For people who are meditating for the first time, a good goal is to try the practice for 5 to 10 minutes every day. If this seems too long or you are having trouble staying focused for the entire time, feel free to shorten it to a comfortable duration. Once you are used to meditating for a certain amount of time, if you would like to increase the duration, simply add one minute at a time and let yourself gradually get used to the new limit. A person should never increase their time until they are able to be still and calm for the entire duration of their meditation without issue.

Before sitting down to meditate, a person should first consider what makes them happy and what they want to visualize during their exercise. This can be in the form of a mantra or a mental picture that helps the person to quiet their mind and feel relaxed. After they establish this, they can consider their goals and what they are hoping to get out of meditating to set their intentions for the session.

One of the most important lessons someone can learn from meditation is patience. It teaches people to be calm and still in the presence of nothingness and that results come in due time. This can sometimes make people uncomfortable at first because society has become so skilled at bombarding people with information all the time, but it is worth learning for inner peace.

It typically takes a few weeks for someone to start noticing the results of their new meditation habit, as long as they are keeping it in their regular routine. The best way to do this is to make it part of a daily ritual such as brushing your teeth or taking a shower. If you can work-in meditation as a mandatory task each day, you are more likely to reap its benefits.

Chapter 13 Meditation of The Present Love

Love is the most powerful emotion to self-heal and feed the soul. Often times, we forget that this amazing feeling is all around us and can be found here this second, without the need of someone else.

As humans, we are naturally able to produce a sense of deep love inside ourselves, before sharing with our partner or with the people we care about. It is not that other people are responsible for our love or for our feeling loved. On the contrary, it is our soul that produces love for others and for itself.

Knowing this, it is easy to understand that there is no need to feel lonely or struggle for a relationship, especially a toxic one. I am not here to tell you that being in a relationship is useless, that is the furthest from the truth and I have always got a lot of value out of being deeply in love with my husband, but I want to reinforce the fact that we can become whole by ourselves. We were not born with a void; we are everything we need to be happy.

This meditation focuses exactly on creating a deep loving sensation inside our soul, that will start the healing process of past traumas.

I recommend doing this meditation consistently for at least one month, in order to see a complete shift in your well-being.

Let's Get Started!

Find a comfortable, relaxed, and balanced position. Give yourself permission to be completely present for yourself, and let your body and mind calm down until they become soft and relaxed.

Breathe in, feel relaxed...
breathe out, feel calm.

Breathe in, feel relaxed...
breathe out, feel calm.

Breathe in, feel relaxed...
breathe out, feel calm.

Breathe in, feel relaxed...
breathe out, feel calm.

Allow the mind to distance itself from all thoughts and orientate awareness on your breath. Breathe naturally and do not force a specific rhythm. Let your breath come and go.

Carefully, now, drive your attention from the breath to the space in which you are.

Feel the energy and atmosphere of this space as it permeates all of your beings. Notice the noises in the background. Maybe there is a clock ticking; maybe there are cars passing just outside your windows. Whatever you feel, it is fine. Let your attention rest on the external.

Breathe in, feel relaxed...
breathe out, feel calm.

Breathe in, feel relaxed...
breathe out, feel calm.

Breathe in, feel relaxed...

breathe out, feel calm.

Breathe in, feel relaxed...
breathe out, feel calm.

Now bring the attention back to the breath. Take your time and you will naturally reach a place of warmth and ease. Stay in this state where you feel your body and mind completely calm, relaxed, and full of peace for a few minutes, without letting go of the focus on your breath.

Breathe in, feel relaxed...
breathe out, feel calm.

Breathe in, feel relaxed...
breathe out, feel calm.

Breathe in, feel relaxed...
breathe out, feel calm.

Breathe in, feel relaxed...
breathe out, feel calm.

Breathe in, feel relaxed...

breathe out, feel calm.

Breathe in, feel relaxed...
breathe out, feel calm.

Breathe in, feel relaxed...
breathe out, feel calm.

Breathe in, feel relaxed...
breathe out, feel calm.

Now, bring your focus to things as they are in the present moment, with a receptive, open, soft attention that does not seek anything in particular, but receives what is there, without rejecting, without aiming for something in particular. Just pay attention to what is around you and to this body here and now.

To help you with this process, you can put your hands on your belly and feel the rhythm of the breath. That is really beneficial, as it will help to direct your attention to a specific part of your body.

Breathe in, feel relaxed...
breathe out, feel calm.
Breathe in, feel relaxed...
breathe out, feel calm.
Breathe in, feel relaxed...
breathe out, feel calm.
Breathe in, feel relaxed...
breathe out, feel calm.
Breathe in, feel relaxed...
breathe out, feel calm.
Breathe in, feel relaxed...
breathe out, feel calm.
Breathe in, feel relaxed...
breathe out, feel calm.
Breathe in, feel relaxed...
breathe out, feel calm.

Now focus your attention on your heart, as that is where love is created. Follow your breath down your nose and your neck, until the air reaches the zone near your heart. Breathe in and out your heart, feeling it becoming bigger and warmer with every single breath.

Allow your mind to build a strong connection with your heart, as each breath now becomes a reason to be loving and be loved by life itself. Let love come to you in a natural way, no matter how long it will take. There is plenty of time for yourself, as nothing worth experiencing arises from the quick and fast.

Just keep breathing in and out your heart, being open to love. I will give you a few minutes; there is no need to rush or to do anything at all.

Breathe in, feel relaxed...
breathe out, feel calm.

Breathe in, feel relaxed...
breathe out, feel calm.

Breathe in, feel relaxed...
breathe out, feel calm.

Breathe in, feel relaxed...
breathe out, feel calm.

Breathe in, feel relaxed...
breathe out, feel calm.

Breathe in, feel relaxed...
breathe out, feel calm.

As you now start feeling the sense of love coming up your heart, notice how every part of your body begins to light up in ecstasy. Your lungs can grasp more air than they used to, your mind is able to reach depths that before were not accessible. Your legs feel a rush of positivity and freshness through them and your hands become way more sensible.

Breathe in, feel relaxed...
breathe out, feel calm.

Breathe in, feel relaxed...
breathe out, feel calm.

Breathe in, feel relaxed...
breathe out, feel calm.

Breathe in, feel relaxed...
breathe out, feel calm.

Breathe in, feel relaxed...
breathe out, feel calm.

Breathe in, feel relaxed...
breathe out, feel calm.

Love is the driving force of the universe, and it is not a surprise that you feel a rush of energy and positivity trough your entire body right now. You are getting in touch with the deepest vibration of the universe, and your entire being is resonating with it. Rest in this blissful sensation, as you are now able to find wisdom in this state of being.

I will give you a few minutes for yourself; there is no need for my words as of now.

Breathe in, feel relaxed...
breathe out, feel calm.

Breathe in, feel relaxed...
breathe out, feel calm.

Breathe in, feel relaxed...
breathe out, feel calm.

Breathe in, feel relaxed...
breathe out, feel calm.

Breathe in, feel relaxed...
breathe out, feel calm.

Breathe in, feel relaxed...
breathe out, feel calm.

Breathe in, feel relaxed...
breathe out, feel calm.
Breathe in, feel relaxed...
breathe out, feel calm.
Breathe in, feel relaxed...
breathe out, feel calm.
Breathe in, feel relaxed...
breathe out, feel calm.
Breathe in, feel relaxed...
breathe out, feel calm.
Breathe in, feel relaxed...
breathe out, feel calm.
Breathe in, feel relaxed...
breathe out, feel calm.
Breathe in, feel relaxed...
breathe out, feel calm.
Breathe in, feel relaxed...
breathe out, feel calm.
Breathe in, feel relaxed...
breathe out, feel calm.
Stay in this beautiful space for as long as you want.
You deserve it.

Breathe in, feel relaxed...
breathe out, feel calm.

Breathe in, feel relaxed...
breathe out, feel calm.

Breathe in, feel relaxed...
breathe out, feel calm.

Breathe in, feel relaxed...
breathe out, feel calm.

Breathe in, feel relaxed...
breathe out, feel calm.

Breathe in, feel relaxed...
breathe out, feel calm.

Breathe in, feel relaxed...

breathe out, feel calm.

Breathe in, feel relaxed...

breathe out, feel calm.

Breathe in, feel relaxed...
breathe out, feel calm.

Breathe in, feel relaxed...
breathe out, feel calm.

Breathe in, feel relaxed...
breathe out, feel calm.

Breathe in, feel relaxed...
breathe out, feel calm.

Breathe in, feel relaxed...
breathe out, feel calm.

Breathe in, feel relaxed...
breathe out, feel calm.

Breathe in, feel relaxed...
breathe out, feel calm.

Breathe in, feel relaxed...
breathe out, feel calm.

Now bring the attention back to the body and start feeling your arms and legs once again. You can close your hands or move your fingers, just to take control of the space around you.

Please, keep the eyes closed for now and enjoy the beautiful moment you are living. You have given yourself the time to feel better and that is absolutely incredible.

Breathe in, feel relaxed...
breathe out, feel calm.

Breathe in, feel relaxed...
breathe out, feel calm.

Breathe in, feel relaxed...
breathe out, feel calm.

Breathe in, feel relaxed...
breathe out, feel calm.

Now become aware of the environment around you once again. Feel the different sounds, the temperature of the room you are in, and once you are ready, open the eyes again.

Chapter 14 Mantra-Based Meditation

One of the quickest ways to benefit from meditation is to use a simple phrase that you keep repeating over and over again. This phrase called mantra is based on ancient Hindu practices. The word "mantra" is related to the concept of holy words. By simply repeating the same statement over and over again, you achieve a meditative state.

Mantra-based meditation strips away the religious and spiritual elements of this traditional practice. You still use a mantra, but instead of a holy word, you use a word that is specifically chosen. You choose a word that has absolutely no meaning to you. This is the key.

How do you know it has no meaning? The right mantra must not conjure up any mental images. When you silently say the word in your mind, you don't feel any sort of judgment-whether good or bad-for the word. Just as important, when you mentally 'say' the word you're considering as a mantra, it doesn't trigger an emotional state.

The whole point of mantra-based meditation is to achieve a mental state where you are not forming thoughts. Well, thoughts could form, but they quickly disintegrate when you repeat your mantra. It's important to note that your mantra isrepeated silently. You don't verbalize it. You don't say it out loud. It's completely quiet. In fact, the best approach is not to engage your vocal muscles at all.

Usually, even when we're thinking, our vocal muscles are still moving because we're trying to mouth out the words. Mantra-based meditation is more effective if you completely skip that process and the word repetition is completely in your mind. It will take some time to override the tendency to 'mouth out' or 'verbally repeat' words. With enough practice, you'll be able to repeat your mantra completely with your mind.

Basic Operations

Mantra-based meditation is based on the traditional practice of transcendental meditation.

It requires a separate space. You have to pick out a space where you can sit in for at least 15 minutes.

It's important that there's enough space so you can sit comfortably. It doesn't have to be an inner room or a dedicated meditation room. Even your office space is fine, as long as you're comfortable and you won't be disturbed for at least 15 minutes.

Posture is crucial.

You have to sit with a fairly straight posture. This is very important. Although you're trying to relax, you don't want to be so relaxed that you end up falling asleep. Some people prefer a lotus sitting position, but this is not absolutely necessary. You can sit on a chair. As long as you're sitting comfortably with your back straight, you should be fine.

It's imperative that you free up a block of time. Budget at least 15 minutes for this. Don't go in less than 15 minutes. Fifteen minutes should do you just fine. Make sure that this block of time is completely freed up. This means turning off your mobile devices and having these 15 minutes completely to yourself.

Your Objective

The objective of mantra-based meditation is to reach a point where your thoughts melt away. This sounds fantastic, but it's actually quite natural. Your mind normally achieves such a relaxed state that thoughts cannot fully form during certain periods of sleep. This is precisely the kind of relaxed state you want your mind to be in.

To achieve this state, you simply begin with paying attention to your breath. Wait a few seconds until you fully exhale, then say your silent mantra. You then inhale slowly until you've filled up your lungs with breath, and then you say your mantra.

It takes a few repetitions of this before you start achieving a relaxed state. You keep it up until the mantra starts breaking up your thoughts. It becomes harder and harder for you to develop a thought. This is crucial because when we pick up on thoughts, we can't help but judge them. We become judgmental. Naturally, these judgments lead to emotional states. We can get worked up—whether positively or negatively, it doesn't matter.

It's really hard to judge or get in an engaged emotional state when you cannot form thoughts. This pays off tremendously if you're having a tough time not reacting to external variables, like if someone looks at you "the wrong way" and you emotionally react in a negative way.

Separating Your Mental and Emotional Processes

Picking up this skill through mantra-based meditation enables you to divorce your thought processes from your emotional processes. With enough practice, you can even divorce sensory inputs from thoughts. You don't have to judge them. You don't have to pick up on them if you don't want to. This leads to a tremendous release from stress. Best of all, you can do this at will!

It's going to be very hard for anything to drag you down, upset you, or otherwise ruffle your feathers. Sounds pretty awesome, right? Well, it's important to start with the right building block. The right building block, of course, is your mantra. It has to be very specifically-chosen.

Quick warning: There are lots of online businesses who claim that they can select a specific personalized mantra for you. Don't fall for such scams. Your mantra can only be chosen by one person: You!

It must be free of any meaning or association for it to work. This can take some time, but the sooner you identify the proper mantra, the more benefits you would get from mantra-based meditation.

I really like this particular meditation method because it is the most effortless of the five methods outlined in this book. In fact, by simply just counting your breath, paying attention to your breathing pattern, and then repeatingyour mantra, you can quickly get into a rhythm.

The rhythm is actually the key to making this meditation technique work. There is no effort to consciously divorce yourself from thoughts because the mantra repetition process itself breaks up your thoughts for you. You simply need to be mindful of the rhythm of your mantra, and everything else would flow from it. Not surprisingly, a lot of people consider mantra-based meditation as one of the 'easiest' forms of meditation.

Many people are drawn to this technique because it's one of the most effortless meditation techniques available. It also works quickly for quite a large percentage of people. I'm not guaranteeing that this would produce the most rapid results in your particular situation. However, if you're like most people and your mind works like most individuals, chances are you can pick this method up fairly quickly and it can produce quite rapid results.

Chapter 15 How to Visualize a Better Version of Yourself

This meditation technique uses your sense of vision. Interestingly enough, you have to use it with your eyes closed. The visual images are being projected through your mind's eye. Imagine your mind having a large projection screen, and you are staring straight into this screen.

Visualization trains you to project certain images to that screen. These images are not emotionally neutral. They pack quite a bit of meaning. You have to be very deliberate and purposeful regarding the images that you choose to project onto that screen because the images lead to certain emotional states.

With enough practice, visualization enables you to conjure up emotional states almost at will. Since you are able to trace the mental image that you form to an emotional trigger, with proper selection of mental habits, you can quickly and efficiently put yourself in a certain emotional state.

Imagine the tremendous amount of control this could give you in your daily waking life. You see, part of the reason many Americans feel that they don't have much control and power over their lives is that they tend to react to external stimuli.

It seems that they are constantly grappling with external stimuli that knock them off track. They know that they have certain values and know that they should act a certain way, but it doesn't take much for external factors to throw them off and react negatively.

Visualization enables you to tap into your power to achieve certain emotional states. For example, if somebody told you that your wife is cheating on you, most guys would react in a very negative way. But suppose you have a tremendous amount of emotional control, thanks to visualization. In that case, you might be able to respond in a way that has a higher probability of leading to less stressful results.

This is a tremendous skill to have because it can pay off in all areas of your life, whether we're talking about your career, your business, your relationships, your general well-being, or even your fitness regimen. The ability to control our emotional state can lead to greater overall success.

At the very least, visualization helps people conjure up a relaxed frame of mind at will. This can come in handy if you're stuck in a stressful situation.

Sadly, most people are creatures of emotional habits. We just need to pick on certain signals for us to respond a certain way, either verbally or physically. If we are not completely clear regarding the kind of emotional states we are confronted with, we almost always react instead of responding based on our higher values.

Basic Operations

To engage in visualization meditation, you just need to find a space where you can sit down in an upright position. It's important that you sit in an upright position so you don't fall asleep while you're visualizing. You then need to close your eyes and think of certain images that you associate with positive states of mind.

Think of images that calm you down. Think of images from your childhood that reassure you. Think of images that give you the reassurance that 'everything will be alright.' Whatever the case may be, most people have distinct and vivid memories of images that trigger a positive emotional cascade.

It's important to be very careful regarding the images you project on your mental screen.

If there is an element of negativity or confusion, this method might not work out as well as you hoped. It's extremely important to be very selective regarding the images that you focus on.

If you pick the right images, you control your mood. This can also trigger a tremendous amount of relaxation. Best of all, you feel conscious throughout the process. You are in complete control because you are the person in charge of the projection device. You are not simply reacting blindly and wildly to whatever random images flash to mind. You control your choice of images.

Turbocharge Your Results With Immersive 3D Effects

While this technique is primarily visual in nature, you don't have to leave it at that level. You can actually increase the amount of emotional clarity and control, as well as inner calm and inner peace that you get from this method by using 3D effects. I am, of course, talking about engaging your other senses.

By simply pairing the mental image that you see with your sense of taste, smell, touch, andhearing, you can make the mental image come to life. The more vivid the image becomes, the stronger the mental and emotional responses you associate with that image are. It becomes more 'real.' If you visualize a very comforting or empowering scene from your childhood, for example, you can't help but feel even more refreshed and reinvigorated by that willful mental image. The image becomes vivid-even palpable. Since your mind interpretsan immersive image as more 'real' than purely visual images, you stand to benefit more fully from the relaxing effects of the right images.

This Method's Best-Selling Point: Experiencing a Creative Explosion

The best-selling point for visualization is that it really explodes your creativity. If you are in any way connected with the arts, this can be a goldmine of creative inspiration. By simply choosing your mental images along with their related emotional states, you can explore your creative side. You can imagine different settings that come to life in a vivid, highly-textured way.

It also awakens your sense of curiosity. This can pay off tremendously, even for business people. A problem that may seem insurmountable might actually be easier to solve than you realize.

Practice, practice, practice

As awesome as visualization sounds, it can only truly work if you practice it consistently.

At first, it can be quite clunky because it requires you to take an inventory of your memories and sort them essentially. However, the more you do this, the faster you get to certain emotional states, and most importantly, the heavier their impact becomes.

Chapter 16 Breath Counting

This is actually one of the oldest forms of meditation. Again, it is rooted in the rich heritage of Buddhist and Hindu spiritual traditions. You are focusing all your mental energy on one particular sensory detail. There is quite a bit of difference, however.

The first difference is that in-breath counting, you have to close your eyes, and the second difference is that here your focus is very predictable. You're focusing on your breath.

To start this practice, you start by counting your breath. You breathe in, breathe out, breathe in, breathe out, and just count your breath.

Next, turn your focus on where the breath leaves your body, which is your nostrils, and then you keep tightening the focus until you zero on the particular area where breath leaves and enters your body. If this sounds familiar, you're absolutely right. There are some elements of this method that are similar to mantra-based meditation. You're essentially using your breathing pattern to trigger a relaxed mental state.

Mental Focus

Once you feel relaxed, the next step is to train your mental camera to speak to the mental images entering your mind. Everybody has mental images. When you're reading a book, there are certain mental pictures that come to mind. When you're listening to somebody in a conversation, there are certain mental images that appear. When you're remembering stuff, mental images form. This is all part of the thinking process. While you're meditating, you're still experiencing these mental images.

The next step of breath counting the single-focus meditation method is to acknowledge these images. Just observe them as they form in your mind. The trick is just to acknowledge them and let them pass. It's like sitting back on a park lawn with your back on the grass and looking up at the blue sky. You would see that the clouds are passing you by and there's no need to capture them. They just pass by overhead.

There's no need to judge these images. Just let them pass you by like clouds. You create a tremendous amount of emotional distance between your thoughts and your emotional state. Also, your mental state is divorced because you are keeping yourself from judging these images.

Breaking Free From Your Tendency to Judge

This is a very important aspect of this meditation practice because when you don't judge, you're not put in a certain emotional state. You just acknowledge these images as they form, get bigger, and then pass. They are then replaced by other mental images and then they pass on.

If you keep this up for a long enough period of time, you'd realize a very powerful truth: You don't have to be thrown off by your thoughts.

You don't have to judge them.
This can lead to a tremendous amount of control because one of the biggest hassles of modern living is to live life in a very reactive way.

If you come across a particular piece of information, it's too easy to get thrown off. It's too easy just to refer it to past bias or past bad experiences. It's too easy to become a prisoner of the past.

Indeed, it's too easy for us to interpret even random or neutral glances from people as hostile or awkward. Every time we talk to people in our communications, there's always an opportunity to interpret whatever they say (or don't say) in the worst way possible. If you do any of these, you are living your life in a reactive way.

Taming the Reactive Mind

When you simply count your breath and learn how to observe mental images and let them pass by without them owning you, you gain a tremendous sense of relief. You let go of your mind's habitual reaction.

This meditation method can lead to relaxation on many different levels. I'm not just talking about physical relaxation. I'm also talking about mental, emotional, and intellectual relaxation.

If you are engaged in the life of the mind, and you get paid to use your brain, it's hard to turn that process off. It's too easy to be intellectually reactive. You are constantly reading stuff into whatever you're experiencing. The more you do this, the more you feel burnt out, but you can't feel you can let go. You feel that if you let go, you lose control.

Ironically, reactive living is a sure sign of loss of personal control.

Breath counting and other singular-sensory-focus-based meditation practices enable you to break free of a reactive mindset.

The secret to this technique is that it pairs a physical singular sensory focus with your thought process. You use the physical focus as a gateway to a higher level of mental mastery and control. As you can probably already tell, this method requires quite a bit of effort. While the amount of control and personal mastery can be quite significant, this method does require quite a bit of premeditation and focus. Depending on your willpower, this can be quite taxing.

The good news is if you stick to it for a long enough period of time, it will get easier. People who prefer this method can actually reach a stage where it becomes second nature. It only takes a few minutes of breath, counting for them to achieve a certain clear, relaxed, and yet empowered mental and emotional state. They can trigger a state of emotional clarity and calm almost at will.

Chapter 17 Anxiety and Stress Relief Scripts

As I mentioned earlier, we all experience anxiety and stress at some point in our lives. In the session to follow, I will help you relieve your anxiety and regain control over your body's automatic response to stressors in your life. These techniques can be used at any point in your day to help you overcome the emotions.

Much like with anything in our lives, practice makes perfect. You should never expect yourself to be perfect at eliminating stress after trying this one time. The more you try, the more improvements you will see when you are dealing with anxiety or stress.

Before we dive into relieving the stress, it is important that you realize the symptoms of anxiety you may be experiencing. For some, you may experience tense muscles, and for others, you may notice rapid breathing. At this moment, you are experiencing none of these. Your body is relaxed and tension free. Your breathing is deep and filling.

In the script to follow, we will target some of these symptoms. This way, when you experience the mentioned symptoms, you will be able to induce the response you are about to learn. To start, I invite you to focus on your breathing and calm yourself.

Now, I invite you to bring your full focus to your breathing. Your breath is going to be key if you are trying to stay relaxed and calm. Take a deep breath in through your nose and slowly exhale through your mouth. Imagine you are blowing out a candle on your birthday cake as you blow the air out of your mouth.

Gently focus on the breath as you inhale. Exhale fully and release all of the air from your lungs. As you breathe in, focus on slowing down the rhythm of your breathing. Tell your breath to be calm, slow, and gentle. Please continue breathing until you feel calm and relaxed.

As you breathe, you are allowing your body to get the oxygen that you need. The only job you have at this moment is to remain relaxed and comfortable. If a stressful thought enters your mind, allow it to pass without judgment. When we fight against anxiety, it only makes it stronger.

If you are feeling anxious at this moment, accept the feeling. Instead of worrying about the emotion, bring your focus back to your thoughts. You are working on being calm. You are breathing and working through these emotions. When you are ready, repeat after me.

I am feeling anxious at this moment, but I am okay. I am feeling anxious, but this feeling will pass.
At this moment, I am safe, even though I feel frightened.

I will continue to breathe and will soon feel calm. I have the ability to get through this.
I have the power to calm my mind and my body.
I have the ability to make myself as comfortable as possible while this feeling passes.

I am in control. I can help myself become calm and relaxed.

This feeling will pass.
As you repeat these phrases, remember to breathe. Breathe in slowly and exhale as you continue to repeat the phrases you need to hear at this moment.

If you are stressed or anxious, you may be experiencing trembling or shaking.

When we are stressed, our body enters fight or flight mode. When we enter this state, our heart beats faster so that our muscles can react if we need to get away from danger. As I mentioned earlier, there is a purpose for our emotions!

If there is no real danger at the moment, there is a lot of adrenaline in your body that is not being used. Due to this adrenaline, your muscles begin to tremble because they are ready for action. You can help decrease this sensation by shaking out the tension.

With this information in mind, bring your focus back to your breath. You are in charge. You have the power to realize that you aren't truly in danger. You are safe in your space right now. Focus on the present and what you have power over.

As you breathe, I invite you to imagine that you are shaking water off of your hands. You gently shake them to get the water off, so you can have dried your hands. Gently shake your hands and allow your hands and wrist to become limp. In your mind's eye, imagine the water flying from your fingertips. As you work gently, the tension you have in your body is leaving and draining from your fingertips.

When you feel your hands are dry, allow your hands to be still. Take a deep breath and exhale. Now, you may notice a pleasant tingling as your hands fall relaxed once again. You have the power to let the tension go.

With the tension gone, it is time to invite calm thoughts back into your mind. Bring your focus back to your breath and calm your heart. Feel it beating gently inside your chest; you are already feeling better and less stressed.

As you continue to breathe, repeat the following phrases after me.

I am becoming calmer.
I am becoming more relaxed. I
am calm.
I am relaxed.
I invite you to repeat these mantras until you believe them in your heart and in your soul.

As we have been discussing your anxiety and stress head-on, you may have noticed tension entering your muscles again. This is a natural reaction when we think of our stress and anxiety. When our muscles are tense, they become painful and tired. Now that you are mindful of your muscles, I will now help you relax again.

First, allow your lower to drop. You will want to make sure that your teeth are no longer touching.

At this moment, inhale and allow your jaw to become loose and relaxed. Exhale.

Next, drop your shoulders from your neck. Try to gently move your shoulders forward and back in small circles. Increase the distance from your shoulders and neck the best you can. I invite you to gently tilt your head from side to side until you feel the tension release from this area.

Now, gently raise your arms above your head. Feel the stretch as your muscles release the tension and then lay them to your sides once again. Bring your head to a neutral and relaxed position. You can continue to move until you feel your muscles have released their tension again. Breathe in and breathe out.

You can keep this exercise in mind any time you feel anxiety or stress creep into your thoughts.

Remember, you can release your anxiety in four short steps.

First, remember to breathe. Keep your breaths full and slow.

Second, keep your thoughts calm. You will want to remind yourself that while you may be feeling this way at the moment, the emotions will pass, and you will be okay.

Third, if your body is shaking, try to physically shake the tension away like water.

Finally, remember to relax your muscles. Take a moment to release your jaw and your shoulders. The sooner you do this, the sooner you will feel better. You can continue these steps until the anxiety leaves you be.

Now, I will go over a general anxiety relaxation exercise with you. If anxiety is something you live with constantly, the following exercise can help you enter a state of physical and mental calm through breath and observing the sensations in your body.

If you wish to help overall anxiety, I suggest doing this relaxation on a regular basis to help you feel calmer in general. When you are a calm person, you may have the ability to withstand stress in a healthier manner. Regular relaxation is the perfect way to protect yourself against the anxiety or stress you may have in your life.

First, take a deep breath in and be sure to fill your lungs.

Breathe out slowly and empty any air you have taken in.

Breathe in... breathe out...
Feel as your breathing keeps you calm and collected at this moment. There is absolutely nothing you need to be worried about right now. There is nowhere to be or nothing to do. All you need is to be here in this moment, enjoying the time you have taken aside for yourself, and fully enjoy this anxiety releasing exercise.

As you continue to breathe, I invite you to turn your attention back to your body. Earlier, we went over the exercise of shaking off your anxiety like water, but I now invite you to notice how you are feeling physically. Do not try to change anything you are feeling at this moment. Instead, try just to be aware of any sensations you have in your body.

However, what you are feeling at this moment is perfectly okay. If something is tense, there is no need to concern yourself over this feeling. If you have unpleasant feelings, recognize that this is most likely from built-up stress. I invite you to scan your body and observe.

Start your scan at your head and move it downward. Notice each area of your body separates from your eyes, your nose, your chin. Each location is going to feel different. Observe each sensation and continue gradually down your body. How is your upper body? How is your stomach feeling after relaxing it from earlier? I invite you to take note of any part of your body still holding onto tension.

Now, move your attention to the lower half of your body. Is there tension in your hips? Remember to observe any tension and move on. We are not trying to change anything in this moment. Take note, and then move down to your legs until you reach the very tip of your toes.

Once your scan is complete, notice how your body feels as a whole. Where is your body most tense? I invite you to focus on one area at the time and imagine the muscles vividly in your mind's eye. Imagine the muscles letting go and becoming relaxed. You have the power to let the tension go bit by bit. Feel the tension in these muscles soften and lengthen. Soon, this area becomes warm and relaxed. Enjoy the new sensation as you let the tension go.

Now, bring your focus to where your body feels most relaxed. Imagine this sensation being warm and tingly, much like with our exercise with your right arm earlier. Now, imagine this sensation growing and spreading to the rest of your body.

As the wave of relaxation washes over your body, you feel both your mind and body coming to complete peace. The air you are breathing brings you relaxation. The air comes through your nose, and you breathe out any tension left in your body.

I invite you to continue breathing. You are releasing the tension and releasing any anxiety you may be experiencing. Notice as the tension in your body is shrinking smaller and smaller until it is almost gone.

Each breath you take in is adding to your relaxation. Your breathing alone can eliminate tension and anxiety altogether. Imagine that you are exhaling any last bit of tension you are holding onto.

Now, you are feeling calm and relaxed. With no tension left, you are breathing in pure relaxation and breathing out relaxation. You are one with this sense of calm and peace.

With this sensation filling you, I invite you to complete another body scan. Try now to imagine that your body is made of chocolate. In this moment, your body is a piece of chocolate, but you can feel the warmth of relaxation filling yourbody.

The warmth starts at your hands and begins to melt your chocolate body. Feel the warmth as it moves from your hands to your arms. The melting is a pleasant feeling, and you are so incredibly relaxed. There is nothing in this world that can bother you; you are so relaxed.

Notice how your legs soften, and your core melts as you become warmer. Now, your whole body is soft. Your chocolate body has melted and become soft. You are floating and relaxing. You have no cares and no anxiety.

Bring your focus back to your thoughts. Notice now that your thoughts have calmed now that you have released the tension from your body and any negative thoughts you may have had earlier. Say goodbye to general anxiety and hello to a new sense of calm.

Breathe in… and breathe out…
It is perfectly normal for our thoughts to wander as we exercise. I invite you to remind yourself to relax. Try to focus your attention on the word "Relax." Repeat this word gently to yourself until you truly believe it. When you are ready, allow your mind to drift again. There is no need to focus on anything specific. You are calm. You are relaxed. You feel released from your anxiety at this moment.

With a slight handle on stress and anxiety, you may feel less anxious already. While these are incredible skills to have on hand for your daily life, you may also feel you need help dealing with panic attacks.

Panic attacks often come on due to stress and anxiety. In the next few exercises, I will give you some mechanisms to help you cope with panic attacks when they happen. Bring your focus back to your breath, and we will begin in a moment.

Chapter 18 The Road to Healing

Healing is a unique experience for everyone who goes through it. For some, it is quick, for others lengthy, and still, others fall somewhere in between. It has to do with the severity of symptoms, willingness to change, and time spent working on reaching goals. Some people are able to achieve their happy ending on their own by reading books like this one or doing their own research and finding techniques that help them manage their anxiety and continue living a normal life. Others might decide they need a little help to make it through a particularly difficult time, and that's okay too.

There are several tricks to manage anxiety and reduce the frequency of panic attacks, and everyone has their own tactic that works best for them. The key to these tips and tricks is to continue trying different ones until a person finds one that works. There are natural remedies such as essential oils, relaxation techniques such as deep breathing, and even cognitive behavioral therapy exercises that can be found online. Not each one of these will work for everyone, though, and people should not be discouraged if they try one method, and it doesn't work for them.

Overcoming fears can be the most difficult part of taking charge of anxiety, but it is also the most important. Avoiding things, a person is afraid of can only make those things seem scarier, but facing them head-on can often take away the mystery and fear. Sometimes, to achieve this, a person will employ a doctor or counselor's help to assist them with developing an action plan and staying on track. This can also help a person more accurately measure their progress and receive feedback from another informed person. This chapter discusses ways a person can manage their anxiety, reduce the frequency of panic attacks, overcome their fears, and ensure their therapy is working for them.

Managing Symptoms

Learning to manage anxiety can be difficult and uncomfortable. It might mean going against all of the signals your brain is sending to face a fear that seems insurmountable. During this time, it is important to remember that working with your doctor to learn new coping skills can be the best and fastest way to start effectively fighting off your anxiety.

The first trick is to learn how to embrace uncertainty. Anxiety can often make someone afraid of the parts of life they don't understand or situations they can't control. Learning to accept that not all things are within your power to manipulate and predict can help you release some of the stress that comes from trying to shape your environment to your needs. Part of embracing uncertainty is being able to recognize when you are obsessing over one thought or worry. Sometimes it can be difficult for anxious people to solve problems or work through logical situations because an anxious thought is spinning around in their brain and dominating their thought process. If they can learn to stop and recognize these thoughts, it can be easier to regain control of their mind and accept that some things are unknown.

Perhaps, the best way to learn and practice these skills is by using mindfulness techniques. Being mindful of yourself and your thoughts can make it much easier to notice when they start erring toward anxiety and away from calm and rational. This way, you can take back control of your thoughts before they spiral too far down the wrong path. These techniques can also reduce worry and increase willpower. If a person is able to tap into their body's needs at any time, it can relax their sense of uncertainty and give them a feeling that they are back in control. These exercises can include setting intentions at the beginning of each day, meditating, going for a walk, or simply looking up at the sky to notice all the things that would normally pass by without a second glance. People can also make a point to put their phones down for an extended period of time to make time to take care of themselves and not have to worry about others. If they want to take this exercise to the next level, they can even leave their phones at home when they go out to experience a release from technology.

One tactic commonly used in cognitive behavioral therapy is to encourage people to realize when their thoughts are distorted. This can be in many ways, such as underestimating their own abilities, predicting negative outcomes, or catastrophizing. If you can start to identify these thoughts for what they are, it is easier to resist the temptation to cave to them and continue with calmness.

It is also important for people to remember that most therapies will not give results right away. They take hard work and dedication to start yielding benefits. Typically, cognitive behavioral therapy takes about 12 to 16 weeks before a person will start seeing marked improvement in their symptoms.

Along with managing their anxiety, a person can also work to reduce the frequency of their panic attacks. Learning to manage panic can be just as stressful as facing fears with anxiety, but once a person can learn to take control of their mind and not be intimidated by their symptoms, having a panic attack might not be the terrible thing it once was.

The first step a person can take to reduce their panic attacks is to make sure they are sticking with the treatment plan their doctor devised withthem. It can be difficult to face things alone once you leave the doctor's office, but make sure you are practicing the techniques he or she teaches you is imperative to success. Sometimes joining a support group can help you to follow through with the action plan. People often find that having a group of others who truly understand and experience the same problems can help them see their issues from a different perspective or find the support they need to continue working toward their goal.

Just like people with anxiety, people who experience frequent panic attacks should limit or avoid exposure to stimulants and depressants such as caffeine, drugs, and alcohol. These substances can make it more difficult to deal with feelings and recognize what your triggers are, so it is best to keep them out of a regular routine.

Stress management tactics are another helpful way to get a grip on panic attacks. People can focus on turning their negative thoughts into positive actions; this might take a little more skill than if someone was dealing with anxiety alone because of the suddenness of panicked thoughts. They can also focus on being assertive instead of aggressive when they are feeling irritated by exercising regularly, and making a schedule to effectively manage their time and tasks.

Relaxation techniques also work equally well for managing panic attacks as with anxiety. Things such as yoga, deep breathing, and muscle relaxation can help the body to calm down even in the face of panicked thoughts or physical symptoms. Making sure you get enough sleep at night is another way to relax the body. Having a bedtime schedule and wake-up times can be incredibly helpful to calm the body because it has a predictable schedule.

If these milder approaches are not doing the trick, sometimes exposure therapy can be the best option for a person to face their fears and decrease the likelihood of a panic attack. This type of therapy involves a person subjecting themselves to the very thing that they are afraid will incite an attack. Typically, this process can be painful the first few times, but after a while, the person will realize the situation does not pose any threat, and there is no reason to feel anxious or panicked.

Some people opt for home remedies to treat panic attacks, especially at their onset. Inhaling lavender essential oils, or putting some in a diffuser, is possibly the most common way people can ease their worry homeopathically. Lavender is known for its calming effects and ability to relax the nervous system.

Moving Forward

An important part of the healing process when someone is overcoming anxiety and panic attacks is to confront their fears. When a person continually avoids things that cause them anxiety, it can cement the fear in their brain and make it more and more intense as time goes on. In order to face their fears, however, a person needs to understand how their brain reacts in scary situations so they can start to identify their triggers and responses. Once they know these two things, staying ahead of the curve can become much easier, and the odds of successfully controlling anxiety can increase.

The first step is to refuse to be afraid of feeling fear. Sometimes the suggestions of fear, such as a trailer for a horror movie, can be enough to get someone's anxiety moving. You can't necessarily avoid commercials for horror movies, though, so a person has to learn that the suggestion of fear and fear itself are two different things. Avoidance can keep a person from doing a number of things in their life, even things they used to enjoy. Fear can be a powerful motivator to stay away from something, but if a person can take a deep breath and acknowledge that it might not spark fear then they could have a better chance of confronting it without anxiety. Exposure therapy usually comes into play after this first step. A person should pick one of their fears that they are motivated to overcome and talk to their doctor about steps to safely expose themselves and become desensitized. Usually, the first time someone practices exposure will be the longest exercise because the trick to this therapy is remaining exposed to the stimulus until the person is able to calm down and feel comfortable. The exercise is repeated over and over once a week or every few days until the person no longer feels afraid of the stimulus. For example, if someone is agoraphobic, their doctor might have someone take them to a grocery store near their home. They would walk around the store until they felt at ease with being in public and around others. This type of therapy helps to teach the brain that what it perceives as a threat is not actually dangerous and the negative outcome it predicted is not real.

People can also overcome their fears by focusing on the positive things in life. You can take a piece of paper and write down all the things you are grateful for to shift your focus onto happiness. It can also be a great reminder of the different people and reasons that make fighting off anxiety worth it. Using humor is also an effective way to lessen anxiety and forget your fears. If someone starts to feel worried, they can make up the most out-of-this-world worst-case scenario, such as aliens landing at the dinner party and there not being enough food to serve all of them, to help them realize how silly some of their worries really are. Learning to appreciate this sense of humor and not taking yourself too seriously can help to reduce stress and anxiety simultaneously.

Even when a person is dedicated to facing their fears and reducing their anxiety, it can still be difficult to do alone. Deciding to start therapy can be a major decision for some people, and once they start, they might not feel like they are making any progress in the beginning. Trusting a therapist can take time, but they are there to support and help you. A therapist can monitor someone's successes and progress and keep them motivated to continue with treatment. Having this consistent, unbiased support can help a person remember that therapy takes time and effort to work.

Most therapists who utilize cognitive behavioral therapy are frequently checking in with their patients and discussing their symptoms, goals, and behaviors. By assessing the person's emotional state and progress, they are able to keep them on track toward achieving their long and short-term goals. This is also how the therapist can make sure that the person is enacting their plan and working on changing their thoughts and behaviors.

If you ever feel concerned that you are not making enough progress while in therapy, you can always ask your doctor to give their opinion. They might discuss with you the steps you've taken in the right direction and things they think might still be holding you back. Most likely, however, they will tell you not to worry because everyone heals at different speeds, and as long as you are putting in the work, you will get the results.

Having a positive relationship with your doctor can also help you feel like you are making progress because it develops trust. It also helps you to open up and let them know all of your symptoms and feelings, so together you can form a comprehensive, realistic action plan that targets them all. When a more detailed action plan can be created, faster results are more likely to occur because the doctor can target very specific things with realistic expectations. This can also help someone trust their doctor more because they see the results they hoped for and acknowledge that hard work is paying off.

Sometimes people want to be able to gauge their success on their own, though, to be able to make their own progress chart. To accomplish this, the first thing you can do is ask yourself how your mood has been impacted by therapy. Has it generally improved, stayed the same, or is it getting worse? If your mood is improving, that can be a good sign that you are improving in small ways also. Another question to ask yourself is if your behaviors have changed since starting therapy. This question can sometimes take a little more self-examination than the first, but it can be another good way to score your progress. A helpful way to measure this is to keep a journal of your reactions to anxious situations so you can see if there are any marked improvements over time.

Finally, a person can also consider whether or not they are solving problems on their own. If they are, this can also indicate that they are working on achieving both their short- and long-term goals.

Conclusion

Thank you for making it through to the end of this book. I hope you found something in this book that has clicked for you; that you had the "ah-ha!" moment that caused you to realize how much power you have. Anxiety and stress are tricky; they show up in daily life and have a sneaky way of making you believe that they are undefeatable. In many ways, your mind is your most powerful tool can also be your worst enemy, and it's all about training your brain to be on your side. Remember to be patient and kind to yourself. You are learning and growing. If it's not troublesome, then it's not making any positive changes in your progress. Remember that your healing process will take time, dedication, and a whole lot of faith in yourself.

Many of us know of pain as an undesirable sensation that arises from infections and injuries. However, pain is also an aftermath of certain disturbances in the brain's normal functions and spinal cord. It can be assumed that the more stable a person's mental state is, the more he or she has the potential to tolerate pain.

More importantly, people who experience anxiety should try to get to the root of their issues. Natural remedies should be seen as treatment, not a cure. People should still work to find out what causes their anxiety, and take the steps necessary to reduce the amount of stress in their lives.

All the natural remedies suggested in this book can be helpful, always know that despite what you think, there are people that want to help you, that want to see you shine and come out on top. But remember, you always have to be there for yourself, even when nobody else is. You're capable; I know you are.

www.ingramcontent.com/pod-product-compliance
Lightning Source LLC
Chambersburg PA
CBHW071612080526
44588CB00010B/1109